Cambridge
BEC Preliminary
2

WITH ANSWERS

Examination papers from University of Cambridge ESOL Examinations: English for Speakers of Other Languages

CAMBRIDGE
UNIVERSITY PRESS

PUBLISHED BY THE PRESS SYNDICATE OF THE UNIVERSITY OF CAMBRIDGE
The Pitt Building, Trumpington Street, Cambridge, United Kingdom

CAMBRIDGE UNIVERSITY PRESS
The Edinburgh Building, Cambridge CB2 2RU, UK
40 West 20th Street, New York, NY 10011–4211, USA
477 Williamstown Road, Port Melbourne, VIC 3207, Australia
Ruiz de Alarcón 13, 28014 Madrid, Spain
Dock House, The Waterfront, Cape Town 8001, South Africa

http://www.cambridge.org

First published 2004

Typeset in Sabon 10.5/12pt and Univers 10/13pt   *System* QuarkXPress™ [s E]

Printed in the United Kingdom at the University Press, Cambridge

ISBN 0 521 544505 Book
ISBN 0 521 54453X Audio Cassette
ISBN 0 521 544521 Audio CD
ISBN 0 521 544513 Self-study Pack

Contents

Thanks and acknowledgements

The authors and publishers are grateful to the following for permission to use copyright material in *BEC Preliminary 2*. While every effort has been made, it has not been possible to identify the sources of all the material used and in such cases the publishers would welcome information from the copyright owners.

p. 78 Extract from 'It is the type of job that sells itself', by Susan MacDonald, published in *The Times*, © NI Syndication, London, 21st September 2000.

Introduction

TO THE STUDENT

This book is for candidates preparing for the Cambridge Business English Certificate Preliminary examination. It contains four complete tests based on past papers.

The BEC Suite

The Business English Certificates (BEC) are certificated examinations which can be taken on various dates throughout the year at approved Cambridge BEC centres. They are aimed primarily at individual learners who wish to obtain a business-related English language qualification, and provide an ideal focus for courses in Business English. Set in a business context, BEC tests English language, not business knowledge. BEC is available at three levels – Preliminary, Vantage and Higher.

The BEC Suite is linked to the five ALTE/Cambridge levels for language assessment, and to the Council of Europe's Framework for Modern Languages. It is also aligned with the UK Qualifications and Curriculum Authority's National Standards for Literacy, within the National Qualifications Framework (NQF).

BEC	Equivalent Main Suite Exam	Council of Europe Framework Level	UK NQF Level
	Certificate of Proficiency in English (CPE)	C2 (ALTE Level 5)	
BEC Higher	Certificate in Advanced English (CAE)	C1 (ALTE Level 4)	Level 2*
BEC Vantage	First Certificate in English (FCE)	B2 (ALTE Level 3)	Level 1
BEC Preliminary	Preliminary English Test (PET)	B1 (ALTE Level 2)	Entry 3
	Key English Test (KET)	A2 (ALTE Level 1)	

* This represents the level typically required for employment purposes to signify the successful completion of compulsory secondary education in the UK.

BEC Preliminary

The BEC Preliminary examination consists of three papers:

Reading and Writing	1 hour 30 minutes
Listening	40 minutes (approximately)
Speaking	12 minutes

Test of Reading and Writing (1 hour 30 minutes)

The **Reading** section of the Reading and Writing paper consists of seven parts with 45 questions, which take the form of two multiple matching tasks, four multiple choice tasks, and a form-filling or note completion task. Part 1 contains five very short texts, Part 2 contains one shorter text and Part 3 contains graphs, charts or tables. Parts 4, 5 and 6 each contain one longer text. Part 7 contains two short texts. The texts are mainly taken from newspapers, business magazines, business correspondence, books, leaflets, brochures, etc. They are all business-related, and are selected to test a wide range of reading skills and strategies.

For the **Writing** section of the Reading and Writing paper, candidates are required to produce two pieces of writing. For Part 1, they write a note, message, memo or email to a colleague or colleagues within the company. For Part 2, they write a piece of business correspondence to somebody outside the company.

Candidates are asked to write 30 to 40 words for Part 1 and 60 to 80 words for Part 2. For Part 1, assessment is based on achievement of task. For Part 2, assessment is based on achievement of task, range and accuracy of vocabulary and grammatical structures, organisation, content and appropriacy of register and format.

Test of Listening (approximately 40 minutes)

This paper consists of four parts with 30 questions, which take the form of two multiple choice tasks and two note completion tasks. Part 1 contains eight very short conversations or monologues, Part 2 contains a short conversation or monologue, Part 3 contains a monologue, and Part 4 contains one longer text. The texts are audio-recordings based on a variety of sources including interviews, telephone calls, face-to-face conversations and documentary features. They are all business-related, and are selected to test a wide range of listening skills and strategies.

Test of Speaking (12 minutes)

The Speaking test consists of three parts, which take the form of an interview section, a short talk on a business topic, and a discussion. In the standard test format, candidates are examined in pairs by two examiners, an interlocutor and an assessor. The assessor awards a mark based on the following four criteria: Grammar and Vocabulary, Discourse Management, Pronunciation and Interactive Communication. The interlocutor provides a global mark for the whole test.

Marks and results

The three BEC Preliminary papers total 120 marks, after weighting. Each skill (Reading, Writing, Listening and Speaking) is weighted to 30 marks. A candidate's overall grade is based on the total score gained in all three papers. It is not necessary to achieve a satisfactory level in all three papers in order to pass the examination. Pass grades are Pass with Merit and Pass. The minimum successful performance in order to achieve a Pass corresponds to about 65% of the total marks. Narrow Fail and Fail are failing grades. Every candidate is provided with a Statement of Results which includes a graphical display of their performance in each skill. These are shown against the scale Exceptional – Good – Borderline – Weak and indicate the candidate's relative performance in each paper.

TO THE TEACHER

Candidature

Each year BEC is taken by over 50,000 candidates throughout the world. Most candidates are either already in work or studying in preparation for the world of work.

Content, preparation and assessment

Material used throughout BEC is as far as possible authentic and free of bias, and reflects the international flavour of the examination. The subject matter should not advantage or disadvantage certain groups of candidates, nor should it offend in areas such as religion, politics or sex.

TEST OF READING

Part	Main Skill Focus	Input	Response	No. of questions
1	Reading – understanding short, real-world notices, messages, etc.	Notices, messages, timetables, adverts, leaflets, etc.	Multiple choice	5
2	Reading – detailed comprehension of factual material; skimming and scanning skills	Notice, list, plan, contents page, etc.	Matching	5
3	Reading – interpreting visual information	Graphs, charts, tables, etc. (The information may be presented in eight separate graphics or combined into a composite graphic.)	Matching	5
4	Reading – for detailed factual information	Longer text (approx. 150–200 words): article, business letter, product description, report, minutes, etc.	Right/Wrong/ Doesn't say	7
5	Reading – for gist and specific information	Longer text (approx. 300–400 words): newspaper or magazine article, advert, report, leaflet, etc.	Multiple choice	6
6	Reading – grammatical accuracy and understanding of text structure	Longer text (approx. 125–150 words): newspaper or magazine article, advert, leaflet, etc.	Multiple choice cloze	12
7	Reading and information transfer	Short memos, letters, notices, adverts, etc.	Form-filling, note completion	5

Reading Part One

In this part there are five short texts, each of which is accompanied by a multiple choice question containing three options. In all cases the information will be brief and clear and the difficulty of the task will lie not in understanding context but in identifying or interpreting meaning.

A wide variety of text types, representative of the world of international business, can appear in this part. Each text will be complete and have a recognisable context.

Preparation
In order to prepare for this part it would be useful to expose students to a wide range of notices and short texts taken from business settings. It is also useful to practise answering sample questions, asking students to explain why the answer is correct (and why the two incorrect options do not apply).

Reading Part Two

This is a matching task comprising one text and five questions, which are often descriptions of people's requirements. Candidates are required to match each question to an appropriate part of the text labelled A–H. (As there are only five questions, some of the labels are redundant.) The testing focus of this part is vocabulary and meaning.

Preparation
For preparation purposes, students need to be familiar with text types that are divided into lists, headings or categories; for example, the contents page of a directory or book, the plan of an office, the departments in a business or shop, the items in a catalogue, etc. Many of the questions in this part require a simple interpretation of what the parts of the text mean and preparation for this could involve setting students real-world tasks of this kind using authentic (but simple) sources.

Reading Part Three

This task consists of eight graphs or charts (or one or more charts or graphs with eight distinct elements) and five questions. Each question is a description of a particular visual and candidates are expected to match the questions to their corresponding graphs, which are labelled A–H.

Preparation
This part focuses on understanding trends and changes. Candidates need to be able to interpret graphic data and understand the language used to describe it. Expressions such as 'rose steadily', 'remained stable', 'decreased slowly', 'reached a peak' should be introduced to students, along with relevant topics, such as sales of goods, share price movement and monthly costs.

Reading Part Four

This task is a text accompanied by seven, three-option multiple choice items. Each question presents a statement and candidates are expected to indicate whether the statement is A 'Right' or B 'Wrong' according to the text, or whether the information is not given in the text (C 'Doesn't say'). Candidates will not be expected to understand every word in the text but they should be able to pick out salient points and infer meaning where words in the text are unfamiliar. The questions will refer to factual information in the text but candidates will be required to do some processing in order to answer the questions correctly.

Preparation
This can be a difficult task for candidates who are not familiar with the three choices represented by A, B and C, and who might not understand the difference between a statement that is incorrect and one that depends on information that is not provided in the text. Students need to be trained to identify a false statement, which means that the opposite or a contradictory statement is made in the text, and to recognise that this is not the same as a statement that is not covered in the text (for which an alternative answer might be 'Don't know').

Reading Part Five

This part presents a single text accompanied by six multiple choice comprehension items. The text is informative and is often taken from a leaflet, or from a newspaper or magazine article.

Candidates are expected to employ more complex reading strategies in this task, in that they should demonstrate their ability to extract relevant information, to read for gist and detail, to scan the text for specific information, and to understand the purpose of the writer and the audience for which the text is intended.

Preparation
In preparing candidates for this part, it would be a good idea to expose them to a variety of texts of a similar length. As texts become longer, slow readers are at a disadvantage and some practice in improving reading speed would be beneficial for this part. It would also be useful to discuss the following areas:
- the title
- the topic
- the writer's purpose
- the theme or main idea of each paragraph
- factual details that can be found in the text
- the writer's opinions (if they are evident).

Reading Part Six

This is a multiple choice cloze test. Candidates have to select the correct word from three options to complete twelve gaps. This part has a predominantly grammatical focus and tests candidates' understanding of the general and detailed meaning of a text and in particular their ability to analyse structural patterns.

Preparation
Any practice in the grammatical and structural aspects of the language is useful in preparing students for this part. However, it is equally important for students to analyse the structure and coherence of language within longer discourse so that they are encouraged to read for meaning beyond the sentence level. As tasks such as this typically focus on common grammatical difficulties, it it also useful to ask students to analyse the errors in their own work. Pairwork activities might be productive as students can often help each other in the areas of error identification and analysis.

Reading Part Seven

Candidates are given two short texts, for example a memo and an advertisement, and are asked to complete a form based on this material. There are five gaps, which should be completed with a word, a number or a short phrase. In this part, candidates are tested on their ability to extract relevant information and complete a form accurately.

For this part, candidates need to transfer their answers in capital letters to an Answer Sheet.

Marks

One mark is given for each correct answer. The total score for Reading is then weighted to 30 marks.

TEST OF WRITING

Part	Functions/Communicative Task	Input	Response	Register
1	e.g. (re-) arranging appointments, asking for permission, giving instructions	Rubric only (plus layout of output text type)	Internal communication (medium may be note, message, memo or email) (30–40 words)	Neutral/ formal/ informal
2	e.g. apologising and offering compensation, making or altering reservations, dealing with requests, giving information about a product	One piece of input which may be business correspondence (medium may be letter, fax or email), internal communication (medium may be note, memo or email), notice, advert, etc. (plus layout of output text type)	Business correspondence (medium may be letter, fax or email) (60–80 words)	Neutral/ formal

For BEC Preliminary, candidates are required to produce two pieces of writing:
● an internal company communication; this means a piece of communication with a colleague or colleagues within the company on a business-related matter, and the delivery medium may be a note, message, memo or email;

- a piece of business correspondence; this means correspondence with somebody outside the company (e.g. a customer or supplier) on a business-related matter, and the delivery medium may be letter, fax or email.

Writing Part One

Candidates are asked to produce a concise piece of internal company communication of between 30 and 40 words, using a written prompt. The text will need to be produced in the form of a note, message, memo or email, and candidates are given guidance on the layout of memos and emails. The reason for writing and target reader are specified in the rubric, and bullet points explain what content points have to be included. Relevant ideas for one or more of these points will have to be 'invented' by the candidate.

Writing Part Two

Candidates are asked to produce an extended piece of business correspondence of between 60 and 80 words. This task involves the processing of a short text, such as a letter or advertisement, in order to respond to it. A number of bulleted content points below the text clearly indicate what should be included in the answer. Some of this information will need to be 'invented' by the candidate.

Although the use of some key words is inevitable, candidates should not 'lift' phrases from the question paper to use in their answers. This may be penalised.

Preparing for the Writing questions

In preparing students for the Writing tasks it would be beneficial to familiarise them with a variety of business correspondence. Analysing authentic correspondence would help students understand better how to structure their answer and the type of language to use. When doing this, it would be useful to focus on the following areas:
- the purpose of the correspondence
- references to previous communication
- factual details
- the feelings and attitude of the writer
- the level of formality
- the opening sentence
- the closing sentence
- paragraphing
- the desired outcome.

If students are in a class, it might be possible to ask them to write and reply to each other's correspondence so that they can appreciate the importance of accurate content.

In a similar fashion, internal company memos and messages might also be written and analysed in terms of the above so that students can recognise the different levels of formality involved. It is a necessary part of preparing for the test that students understand the uses of, and styles inherent in, different types of business communication so that they are aware of how and why different types of correspondence are used.

Assessment

An impression mark is awarded to each piece of writing. For each task, a general impression mark scheme is used in conjunction with a task-specific mark scheme, which focuses on criteria specific to each particular task.

For Part 1, examiners use the mark schemes primarily to assess task achievement. For Part 2, examiners use the mark schemes to assess both task achievement **and** language.

The band scores awarded are translated to a mark out of 5 for Part 1 and a mark out of 10 for Part 2. The total score for Writing is then weighted to 30 marks.

Both general impression mark schemes are interpreted at Council of Europe Level B1.

Summaries of the general impression mark schemes are reproduced below. Examiners work with a more detailed version, which is subject to regular updating.

General mark scheme for Writing Part One

Band	
5	**Very good attempt** at task, achieving all content points.
4	**Good attempt** at task, achieving all content points.
3	**Satisfactory attempt** at task, achieving all content points with some effort by the reader, or achieving two content points.
2	**Inadequate attempt** at task, achieving one content point, possibly with noticeable irrelevance.
1	**Poor attempt** at task; no content points achieved, has little relevance.
0	No relevant response or too little language to assess.

General mark scheme for Writing Part Two

Band	
5	Full realisation of the task set. ● All four content points achieved. ● Confident and ambitious use of language; errors are minor, due to ambition, and non-impeding. ● Good range of structure and vocabulary. ● Effectively organised, with appropriate use of simple linking devices. ● Register and format consistently appropriate. Very positive effect on the reader.
4	Good realisation of the task set. ● Three or four content points achieved. ● Ambitious use of language; some non-impeding errors. ● More than adequate range of structure and vocabulary. ● Generally well organised, with attention paid to cohesion. ● Register and format on the whole appropriate. Positive effect on the reader.
3	Reasonable achievement of the task set. ● Three content points achieved. ● A number of errors may be present, but are mostly non-impeding. ● Adequate range of structure and vocabulary. ● Organisation and cohesion are satisfactory, on the whole. ● Register and format reasonable, although not entirely successful. Satisfactory effect on the reader.
2	Inadequate attempt at the task set. ● Two or three content points achieved. ● Numerous errors, which sometimes impede communication. ● Limited range of structure and vocabulary. ● Content is not clearly organised or linked, causing some confusion. ● Inappropriate register and format. Negative effect on the reader.
1	Poor attempt at the task set. ● One or two content points achieved. ● Serious lack of control; frequent basic errors. ● Little evidence of structure and vocabulary required by task. ● Lack of organisation, causing a breakdown in communication. ● Little attempt at appropriate register and format. Very negative effect on the reader.
0	Achieves nothing. Either fewer than 25% of the required number of words or totally illegible or totally irrelevant.

TEST OF LISTENING

Part	Main Skill Focus	Input	Response	No. of questions
1	Listening for specific information	Short conversations/monologues	3-option multiple choice	8
2	Listening for specific information	Short telephone conversation/prompted monologue	Gap-filling (numbers and spellings)	7
3	Listening for specific information	Monologue	Note-taking (content words)	7
4	Listening for gist/specific information	Conversation/Interview/Discussion between two or more people	3-option multiple choice	8

Listening Part One

The eight questions in this part of the paper are three-option multiple choice questions. For each question, candidates hear a short conversation or monologue, typically lasting around 15 to 30 seconds. Each monologue or dialogue is repeated on the tape in order to give candidates a chance to check their answer. The multiple choice options may be textual or they may be in the form of pictures, graphs or diagrams.

In the extracts in Part 1 candidates are being tested on their understanding of spoken English used in a range of situations and on their ability to extract factual information. They may need to pick out a name or time or place. Alternatively, they may have to identify a trend in a graph or a place on a map or the location of an object in a room. In every case it will be necessary for candidates to follow the conversation closely.

Listening Part Two

This part consists of a short conversation or monologue, typically lasting around a minute and a half, which contains factual information. On the question paper there is a form, table, chart or set of notes with seven gaps where information is missing. Candidates have to complete each of the gaps. This part has a numerical focus and the answers may include dates, prices, percentages or figures.

Listening Part Three

Candidates hear a monologue. On the question paper there is a set of notes or a form with gaps. There are seven gaps to complete and the answers may be one or two words. On occasion, the key to one of the gaps may be a date.

Listening Part Four

This part, which lasts about three minutes, contains a longer listening text which generally takes the form of an interview, or a discussion between two or possibly more speakers. There are eight, three-option multiple choice questions on the question paper and these are always in a written format. In this part of the Listening component candidates are being tested on their ability to understand the gist of a longer text and extract detailed and specific information as required by the questions. They may also be tested on the speakers' opinions.

At the end of the Listening test, candidates have ten minutes to transfer their answers to their Answer Sheet.

Preparing for the Listening paper

The Listening component is carefully paced and candidates are tested on short extracts in Part 1 so that they can gradually 'tune in' to the spoken language and improve their listening skills without losing their place in the test.

Listening can be a very demanding activity and candidates should practise their listening skills regularly using a wide variety of listening sources. Candidates who enter the Listening test having done this will be at an advantage.

At BEC Preliminary level, it is advisable to collect as much listening material as possible that is suitably paced and of an appropriate length. Native speakers speak at many different speeds and some speak much more clearly than others. If it is possible to collect a bank of authentic material that is carefully chosen, this would prove useful practice for students. Otherwise it might be better to make use of specially designed materials for this level.

For Part 1, candidates should try to listen to short extracts of speech concentrating on understanding the general idea or main points of what is said. For Parts 2 and 3, practice should be given in note-taking. Prior to hearing tapes or audio materials, students should be given details of the information they need to listen for. Teachers should discuss the task with the students beforehand and encourage them to listen for cues and prompts that will help them identify the points they need to find. When listening to longer texts, it would also be useful to discuss areas such as:
- the purpose of the speech or conversation
- the speakers' roles
- the speakers' opinions
- the language functions being used
- factual details
- conclusions.

Marks

One mark is given for each correct answer, giving a total score of 30 marks for the whole Listening paper.

TEST OF SPEAKING

Part	Format/Content	Time	Interaction Focus
1	Conversation between the interlocutor and each candidate General interaction and social language	About 2 minutes	The interlocutor encourages the candidates to give information about themselves and to express personal opinions
2	A 'mini presentation' by each candidate on a business theme Organising a larger unit of discourse Giving information and expressing opinions	About 5 minutes	The candidates are given prompts which generate a short talk on a business-related topic
3	Two-way conversation between candidates followed by further prompting from the interlocutor. Expressing opinions, agreeing and disagreeing	About 5 minutes	The candidates are presented with a scenario supported by visual or written prompts which generates a discussion The interlocutor extends the discussion with further spoken prompts

Speaking Part One

In the first part of the test, the interlocutor addresses each candidate in turn and asks questions about where they work or study, where they live or what they do in their free time. The questions will be slightly different for each candidate and candidates will not be addressed in strict sequence. This part of the test lasts about two minutes and during this time candidates are being tested on their ability to talk briefly about themselves, to provide information on subjects such as their home, hobbies and jobs, and to perform simple functions such as agreeing and disagreeing, and expressing preferences.

Speaking Part Two

The second part of the test is a 'mini presentation'. Candidates are asked to speak for about one minute on a business-related topic. At Preliminary level candidates are given two topics from which they should choose **one**. Each topic is presented as a main focus with three bullet points. Candidates are given one minute to prepare the talk (both candidates or group of three prepare at the same time). After each candidate finishes speaking the next candidate is asked which of the bullet points they think is the most important. This part of the test focuses on the candidate's ability to present basic ideas and organise a longer piece of discourse.

Speaking Part Three

The third part of the test is a two-way conversation (three-way in a three-candidate format) between candidates. The interlocutor outlines a scenario and provides prompts by way of black and white pictures or written prompts to help the candidates. The candidates are asked to speak for about two minutes. The interlocutor will support the conversation as appropriate and then ask further questions related to the main theme. This part of the test focuses on the candidate's ability to interact appropriately using a range of linguistic skills.

Preparing for the Speaking test

It is important to familiarise candidates with the format of the test before it takes place, by the use of paired activities in class. Teachers may need to explain the benefits of this type of assessment to candidates. The primary purpose of paired assessment is to sample a wider range of discourse than can be elicited from an individual interview.

In the first part of the test, candidates mainly respond to questions or comments from the interlocutor. In the second part, candidates are given the opportunity to produce an extended piece of discourse and to demonstrate an ability to maintain a longer speech turn. In the third part, they are required to interact more actively, taking turns appropriately, asking and answering questions and negotiating meaning. To prepare for this part, it is a good idea to encourage students to change partners in class so that they grow accustomed to interacting with a variety of people, some of whom they do not know so well.

For all parts of the test students need to practise the exchange of personal and non-personal information, and prompt materials will be needed to help them do this. Teachers could prepare a selection of these for each part of the test. Students could discuss the materials as a class group prior to engaging in pairwork activities. Such activities would familiarise students with the types of interactive skills involved in asking and providing factual information, such as: speaking clearly, formulating questions, listening carefully and giving precise answers.

Assessment

Candidates are assessed on their own performance and not in relation to each other according to the following analytical criteria: Grammar and Vocabulary, Discourse Management, Pronunciation and Interactive Communication. These criteria are interpreted at Preliminary level. Assessment is based on performance in the whole test.

Both examiners assess the candidates. The assessor applies detailed, analytical scales, and the interlocutor applies a Global Achievement Scale which is based on the analytical scales. The analytical criteria are further described below.

Grammar and Vocabulary

This refers to range and accuracy as well as the appropriate use of grammatical and lexical forms. At BEC Preliminary, a range of grammar and vocabulary is needed to deal with the tasks. At this level, candidates may make frequent minor errors and use some inappropriate vocabulary, but this should not obscure intended meanings.

Discourse Management

This refers to the coherence, extent and relevance of each candidate's individual performance. Contributions should be adequate to deal with the tasks. At times, candidates' utterances may be inappropriate in length and some utterances may lack coherence.

Pronunciation

This refers to the candidate's ability to produce comprehensible utterances. At BEC Preliminary, most meanings are conveyed through the appropriate use of stress, rhythm, intonation and clear individual sounds, although there may be some strain on the listener.

Interactive Communication

This refers to the candidate's ability to take an active part in the development of the discourse. At BEC Preliminary, candidates are able to take turns and sustain the interaction by initiating and responding appropriately. Hesitation may demand patience of the listener.

Global Achievement Scale

This refers to the candidate's overall performance throughout the test. Throughout the Speaking test candidates are assessed on their language skills and, in order to be able to make a fair and accurate assessment of each candidate's performance, the examiners must be given an adequate sample of language to assess. Candidates must, therefore, be prepared to provide full answers to the questions asked by either the interlocutor or the other candidate, and to speak clearly and audibly. While it is the responsibility of the interlocutor, where necessary, to manage or direct the interaction, thus ensuring that both candidates are given an equal opportunity to speak, it is the responsibility of the candidates to maintain the interaction as much as possible.

Grading and results

Grading takes place once all scripts have been returned to Cambridge ESOL and marking is complete. This is approximately five weeks after the examination. There are two main stages: grading and awards.

Grading

The three papers total 120 marks, after weighting. Each skill represents 25% of the total marks available. The grade boundaries (Pass with Merit, Pass, Narrow Fail and Fail) are set using the following information:
- statistics on the candidature
- statistics on the overall candidate performance

- statistics on individual items, for those parts of the examination for which this is appropriate (Reading and Listening)
- the advice of the Chief Examiners, based on the performance of candidates, and on the recommendation of examiners where this is relevant (Writing)
- comparison with statistics from previous years' examination performance and candidature.

A candidate's overall grade is based on the total score gained in all three papers. It is not necessary to achieve a satisfactory level in all three papers in order to pass the examination.

Awards

The Awarding Committee deals with all cases presented for special consideration, e.g. temporary disability, unsatisfactory examination conditions, suspected collusion, etc. The committee can decide to ask for scripts to be re-marked, to check results, to change grades, to withhold results, etc. Results may be withheld because of infringement of regulations or because further investigation is needed. Centres are notified if a candidate's results have been scrutinised by the Awarding Committee.

Results

Results are reported as two passing grades (Pass with Merit and Pass) and two failing grades (Narrow Fail and Fail). Candidates are given Statements of Results which, in addition to their grades, show a graphical profile of their performance on each paper. These are shown against the scale Exceptional – Good – Borderline – Weak and indicate the candidate's relative performance in each paper. Certificates are issued to passing candidates after the issue of Statements of Results and there is no limit on the validity of the certificate.

Further information

For more information about BEC or any other Cambridge ESOL examination write to:

Cambridge ESOL Information
1 Hills Road
Cambridge CB1 2EU
United Kingdom

Tel: +44 1223 553355
Fax: +44 1223 460278
email: ESOL@ucles.org.uk
website: www.CambridgeESOL.org

In some areas, this information can also be obtained from the British Council.

Test 1

READING AND WRITING   1 hour 30 minutes

READING

PART ONE

Questions 1–5

- Look at questions **1–5**.
- In each question, which sentence is correct?
- For each question, mark one letter (**A**, **B** or **C**) on your Answer Sheet.

Example: 0

> Don't forget –
>
> flight BA692   6.45 pm

The plane arrives at

A   quarter to seven in the morning.
B   quarter past six in the evening.
C   quarter to seven in the evening.

The correct answer is **C**, so mark your Answer Sheet like this:

1

> Item 20 in this catalogue is withdrawn until further notice,
> due to supply problems.

A   Item 20 is now discontinued.
B   Item 20 has developed a fault.
C   Item 20 is unavailable at the moment.

2

> **Jane Halton, currently Finance Director at Curtis Bank, is replacing**
> **John Murphy as Chief Executive at Boulder Insurance**

A   Jane Halton is moving from banking to insurance.
B   Boulder Insurance hopes to appoint a new Chief Executive.
C   The post of Chief Executive at Curtis Bank has become vacant.

3

The London Centre

for your meeting, product launch, special event

◆ Purpose-built rooms

◆ Latest presentation technology

◆ First-class food

This organisation

A   rents luxury office space.
B   provides conference facilities.
C   markets other companies' goods.

4

FINEFOODS

Agent required for nationwide distribution.
Some experience in food retail an advantage.
Refrigerated van provided.

Finefoods requires an agent to

A   own a suitable vehicle for delivery.
B   be a specialist in food distribution.
C   deliver goods all over the country.

5

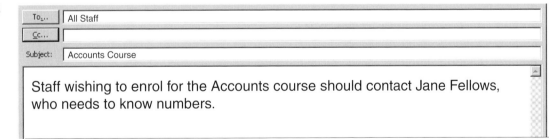

Staff should tell Jane Fellows

A   how many people have enrolled for the course.
B   if they are interested in doing the course.
C   which of the courses they have decided to do.

PART TWO

Questions 6–10

- Look at the list below. It shows a number of business training courses.
- For questions **6–10**, decide which training course (**A–H**) each person on the opposite page needs.
- For each question, mark one letter (**A–H**) on your Answer Sheet.
- Do not use any letter more than once.

TILLERS PROFESSIONAL DEVELOPMENT COURSES

A Decision-making at board level

B Making maximum use of older hardware

C Working with other managers

D Handling difficult situations in the workplace

E Updating IT skills for advertising

F Dealing with customer complaints

G Managing your own time efficiently

H Improving productivity in the factory

6   Office manager Helen Turner needs to deal with complaints from staff about some colleagues' use of email.

7   Before deciding to buy a new computer, David Thompson wants to find out whether he can update his existing equipment.

8   Claire Collier's toy company has a major new customer and she needs to manufacture more goods without increasing staffing levels.

9   Publicity manager Brian Steward did a computer course several years ago, and now wants to learn about developments relevant to his field.

10 Richard Masters was recently promoted and would like to improve his ability to meet deadlines.

PART THREE

Questions 11–15

- Look at the chart below. It shows a company's performance on the London stock market during 10 working days.
- Which day does each sentence (**11–15**) on the opposite page describe?
- For each sentence, mark one letter (**A–H**) on your Answer Sheet.
- Do not use any letter more than once.

STOCK MARKET PERFORMANCE

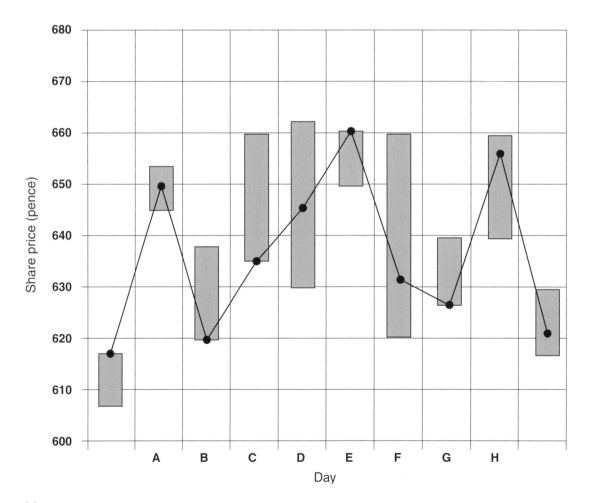

11 At the close of this day's trading, shares dipped just below 630 pence, despite achieving higher levels throughout the rest of the day.

12 On this day share prices closed considerably lower than the previous working day, with the fluctuation between high and low being at its greatest.

13 Shares closed at their lowest value of the day's trading, but narrowly avoided the worst performance of the period.

14 Shares closed at a higher value than the previous two days, although around 17 pence down on the high point for the day.

15 During this day shares rose and fell within only a narrow margin and closed in the middle of the range, before falling sharply at the end of the following day.

PART FOUR

Questions 16–22

- Read the article below about a self-employed journalist.
- Are sentences **16–22** on the opposite page 'Right' or 'Wrong'? If there is not enough information to answer 'Right' or 'Wrong', choose 'Doesn't say'.
- For each sentence (**16–22**), mark one letter (**A, B** or **C**) on your Answer Sheet.

Sally Patterson, journalist

Last year, Sally Patterson left her permanent job with a newspaper and is now a self-employed journalist. Why did she do it? 'I had no control over my work,' she says, 'and that mattered more to me than earning lots of money. Actually, leaving my job wasn't as difficult as I'd expected, because I already had plenty of contacts in the publishing industry. Unlike my last job, though, I'm mostly in touch with the magazines and newspapers I write for by email, and as I don't work in an office, I may not see anyone for days. But that's a welcome relief!'

Isn't it hard being self-employed? 'The biggest danger when you become self-employed is saying "yes" to everything,' Sally says. 'I make sure I turn work down if I haven't got the time for it. And that's a question of planning: I spend an hour every week working out what I'm doing for the next few months.'

And what about the benefits? 'Well, at the newspaper I always concentrated on economic matters, but now I can choose to work on a wider range of projects than before. And being my own boss has made me feel more confident about the other areas of my life, too.'

16 Sally left her last job because she wanted to make decisions about her work herself.

   A Right   **B** Wrong   **C** Doesn't say

17 Her colleagues in publishing thought that being self-employed would be difficult for her.

   A Right   **B** Wrong   **C** Doesn't say

18 She would prefer to share an office with other people.

   A Right   **B** Wrong   **C** Doesn't say

19 She needs to accept all the work she is offered.

   A Right   **B** Wrong   **C** Doesn't say

20 Most self-employed journalists find it difficult to plan ahead.

   A Right   **B** Wrong   **C** Doesn't say

21 Sally specialises more now than she did in her last job.

   A Right   **B** Wrong   **C** Doesn't say

22 Self-employment has affected Sally's attitude to life.

   A Right   **B** Wrong   **C** Doesn't say

PART FIVE

Questions 23–28

- Read the article below about a company which repairs turnstiles (the metal gates used at sports grounds).
- For each question (**23–28**) on the opposite page, choose the correct answer.
- Mark one letter (**A**, **B** or **C**) on your Answer Sheet.

Master of the turnstiles

For years Jim Cartwright enjoyed spending his spare time repairing his local football club's turnstiles, the metal gates which allow one person at a time into the football ground. When Jim was made redundant from his full-time job selling equipment to sports organisations, he realised he already knew plenty of people responsible for turnstiles. This made him sure that his hobby could become a successful new career.

He had 1000 brochures printed and posted them to clubs around the country. For two weeks he heard nothing. Then Troon Football Club requested a quotation for repairing their turnstiles, with the possibility of the work becoming regular. He wanted the contract so much that he cut his profit margin to a minimum. He won it, though

with no guarantee of further work, and celebrated the launch of his new business.

In the next month, club after club offered Jim work, and he recruited his first employee, Alec, to help re-install the repaired turnstiles. Alec, however, took frequent breaks and never put in more effort than he had to. What's more, he seemed unhappy working for Jim. Although Jim had no complaints about the quality of his work, Alec's attitude made him difficult to work with.

Jim considered dismissing Alec, but recruiting him had taken a long time because there had been so many suitable people to interview. Now he was simply too busy to go through that process again. And anyway, Jim had employed Alec on the understanding that the job would probably end when the current contracts were completed.

Suddenly, though, Jim's business was at risk. He made very few mistakes, and calculated his costs and the time that a job would take very accurately. But he had forgotten that generally clubs have repairs done between the end of one football season and the start of the next. Now no major jobs were coming in.

After buying a replacement van, as his old one was beyond repair, he could only just cover Alec's wages and his own. But without more work he had no future. The solution was something more regular, and he decided to produce turnstiles, as well as repair them. For an investment like this, though, he needed help, and he persuaded his bank to give him a loan. From then on, Cartwright Turnstile Services just grew and grew and now employs three full-time workers.

23 Why was Jim Cartwright confident about starting a business repairing turnstiles?

    A   He had learnt from mistakes that his previous employer made.

    B   He had a lot of contacts with possible customers.

    C   He had experience of doing the work in his previous job.

24 Why was Jim happy that Troon Football Club gave him the contract?

    A   It was the first his firm had received.

    B   It led to long-term work for the club.

    C   It provided him with a good profit.

25 What problem did Jim have with Alec?

    A   His work was not of a high enough standard.

    B   He did as little work as possible.

    C   He made a lot of complaints about the business.

26 Why did Jim decide to continue employing Alec?

    A   It would take too long to find a replacement.

    B   There was a lack of people with the right qualifications.

    C   Jim had given him a contract which guaranteed him work.

27 Why did Jim find himself in danger of going out of business?

    A   His costs were higher than he had estimated.

    B   He found that each job took longer than he expected.

    C   His work was mostly limited to certain times of year.

28 Jim asked his bank for a loan in order to

    A   pay the wages bill.

    B   start manufacturing.

    C   buy a new van.

PART SIX

Questions 29–40

- Read the information leaflet below about an exhibition.
- Choose the correct word to fill each gap, from **A**, **B** or **C** on the opposite page.
- For each question (**29–40**), mark one letter (**A**, **B** or **C**) on your Answer Sheet.

CORPORATE TRAVEL EXHIBITION

This year's Corporate Travel exhibition will take place on 13 and 14 October. The exhibition is twice the size it was last year (**29**) .... the organisers have been successful in attracting many more (**30**) .... airlines, hotels and car rental companies than in the past. (**31**) .... 150 companies will have stands (**32**) .... the exhibition.

During the two days of the exhibition, (**33**) .... will be a programme of seminars (**34**) .... a wide range of subjects related to business travel. Each of (**35**) .... will provide professional advice on ways in (**36**) .... firms can obtain a high level (**37**) .... service at the most competitive prices. Participants will have the opportunity to learn (**38**) .... to achieve savings of up to 40% on (**39**) .... annual travel budgets.

The exhibition will be open 10.00–17.00 on (**40**) .... days.

29	**A**	if	**B**	when	**C**	as
30	**A**	leading	**B**	first	**C**	primary
31	**A**	Above	**B**	Over	**C**	Ahead
32	**A**	with	**B**	on	**C**	at
33	**A**	there	**B**	one	**C**	it
34	**A**	cover	**B**	covers	**C**	covering
35	**A**	this	**B**	these	**C**	that
36	**A**	which	**B**	what	**C**	where
37	**A**	for	**B**	of	**C**	to
38	**A**	how	**B**	why	**C**	whether
39	**A**	them	**B**	they	**C**	their
40	**A**	either	**B**	both	**C**	every

PART SEVEN

Questions 41–45

- Read the email and the note below.
- Complete the form on the opposite page.
- Write a word or phrase (in CAPITAL LETTERS) or a number on lines **41–45** on your Answer Sheet.

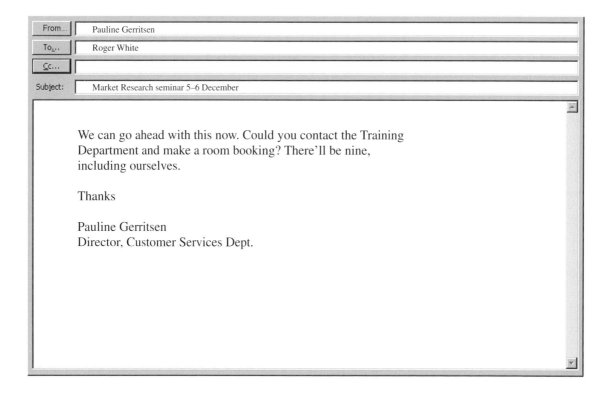

From...	Pauline Gerritsen
To...	Roger White
Cc...	
Subject:	Market Research seminar 5–6 December

We can go ahead with this now. Could you contact the Training Department and make a room booking? There'll be nine, including ourselves.

Thanks

Pauline Gerritsen
Director, Customer Services Dept.

Mary,

Could you book a room for the market research seminar in my name and let me have a copy of the form?
We usually have an oval table. We'll bring our own laptop, but to display the figures we'll need a large screen.
Call me if there's any problem.

Roger

P.S. Don't forget to ask for parking spaces!

Room Bookings

BOOKING REQUESTED BY: **(41)** .... Department

NAME OF CONTACT: **(42)** ....

DATE(S):   5–6 December

NUMBER OF PEOPLE: 9

FURNITURE REQUIRED: **(43)** ....

EQUIPMENT REQUIRED: **(44)** ....

OTHER REQUESTS: **(45)** ....

WRITING

PART ONE

Question 46

- Your line manager asked you to write a report on your latest sales figures. Unfortunately, it is not ready yet.
- Write an **email** to your manager:
  - apologising for the delay
  - giving the reason for the delay
  - saying when the report will be ready.
- Write **30–40** words on your Answer Sheet.

To...	
Cc...	
Subject:	Sales Report

PART TWO

Question 47

- Read the part of a letter below from Ms Lambert, the Bookings Coordinator at a business training centre.

We run the Business Management course twice a year, 3rd–7th January and 5th–9th June.

We advise delegates to reserve places well in advance of the course start date.

Please let me know as soon as possible the number of people attending and which dates you prefer, in order to ensure your reservation.

- Write a **letter** to Ms Lambert:
  - thanking her for her letter
  - saying how many people will be on the course
  - explaining why you cannot give her the course date yet
  - enquiring about discounts.
- Write **60–80** words on your Answer Sheet.
- Do not include any postal addresses.

LISTENING   Approximately 40 minutes (including 10 minutes' transfer time)

LISTENING

PART ONE

Questions 1–8

- For questions **1–8** you will hear eight short recordings.
- For each question, mark **one** letter (**A**, **B** or **C**) for the correct answer.

Example:

When were the machine parts sent?

Monday 31	Tuesday 1	Thursday 3
A	**B**	**C**

The answer is **A**.

- After you have listened once, replay each recording.

1   Why does the woman want the job?

    A   to reduce travel time
    B   to learn about computers
    C   to earn more money

2   When is the trade fair?

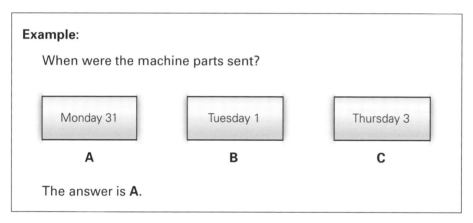

    A   **B**   **C**

3   What is the purpose of today's meeting?

    A   to discuss a merger plan
    B   to obtain some advice
    C   to sign a contract

4   Which chart shows this year's sales?

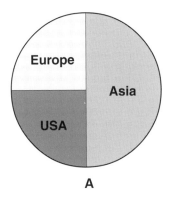 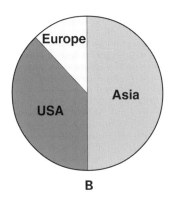 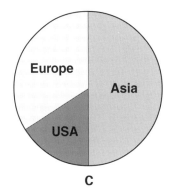

           A   **B**   **C**

5   How much will Emma's hotel bill be?

£60.00	£65.50	£72.50
A	**B**	**C**

6   What will the finance company give advice about?

    A   buying shares
    B   setting up a small business
    C   paying less tax

7 Which graph are they looking at?

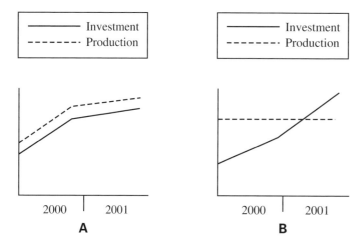
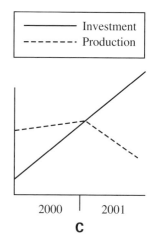

A   **B**   **C**

8 What's the problem with the seminar?

 A the speaker's availability
 B the size of the room
 C the low number of bookings

PART TWO

Questions 9–15

- Look at the notes below.
- Some information is missing.
- You will hear a man telephoning a sports centre.
- For each question (**9–15**), fill in the missing information in the numbered space using a **word**, **numbers** or **letters**.
- After you have listened once, replay the recording.

Ace Sports Centre – Customer Details

CUSTOMER NAME: (9) Charles ....

COMPANY NAME: (10) .... Ltd

MEMBERSHIP NUMBER: (11) ....

DATE OF GROUP INTRODUCTION: (12) .... November

DISCOUNT OFFERED: (13) .... %

CONTACT NUMBER: (14) 01332 ....

EMAIL ADDRESS: (15) info@.................................... .com

PART THREE

Questions 16–22

- Look at the notes below.
- Some information is missing.
- You will hear part of a report by the company's chairman.
- For each question (**16–22**), fill in the missing information in the numbered space using **one** or **two** words.
- After you have listened once, replay the recording.

Concept Trading Inc.

Appointment of new MD: (16) Bob ....

Top-selling product in
2001: (17) ....

Largest growth seen in
sales of (18) .... furniture

Most successful branch: (19) ....

Future Plans - 2003

Introduction of (20) ....

Open 6 stores in (21) .... centres

New subject for staff
training programme: (22) ....

PART FOUR

Questions 23–30

- You will hear a discussion between two managers, Matthew and Angela, about some problems with staff.
- For each question (**23–30**), mark **one** letter (**A**, **B** or **C**) for the correct answer.
- After you have listened once, replay the recording.

23   How many junior managers resigned in June?

    A   one
    B   two
    C   three

24   Matthew thinks the junior managers are leaving because

    A   they don't like working in the company.
    B   they want to get wider experience.
    C   they can earn more in other companies.

25   What does Matthew think about junior managers who resign?

    A   They need to leave to get promotion.
    B   They should be more patient.
    C   They are bad at their jobs.

26   What does Angela find most annoying about hiring new staff?

    A   reading so many CVs
    B   interviewing applicants
    C   training the new staff

27   Matthew was told that taking on the wrong person can

    A   make other staff want to leave.
    B   create extra work for the team.
    C   cause the company to lose money.

28   What is the Personnel Department thinking about using?

   A   employment agencies
   B   personality tests
   C   handwriting experts

29   Matthew thinks handwriting tests do not show if people are

   A   intelligent.
   B   ambitious.
   C   confident.

30   Matthew and Angela agree that the company should

   A   ask for more details on application forms.
   B   review its advertisements for vacancies.
   C   change the way candidates are interviewed.

You now have 10 minutes to transfer your answers to your Answer Sheet.

SPEAKING   12 minutes

PART ONE

The interview – about 2 minutes

In this part the interlocutor asks questions to each of the candidates in turn. You have to give information about yourself and express personal opinions.

PART TWO

'Mini presentation' – about 5 minutes

In this part of the test you are asked to give a short talk on a business topic. You have to choose one of the topics from the two below and then talk for about one minute. You have one minute to prepare your ideas.

A   WHAT IS IMPORTANT WHEN . . .?

JOINING A COMPUTER SKILLS COURSE

- COURSE MATERIALS
- TRAINER
- NUMBER OF PARTICIPANTS IN GROUP

B   WHAT IS IMPORTANT WHEN . . .?

CHOOSING A DELIVERY COMPANY

- SPEED OF SERVICE
- COST
- PERSONAL RECOMMENDATION

PART THREE

Discussion – about 5 minutes

In this part of the test the examiner reads out a scenario and gives you some prompt material in the form of pictures or words. You have 30 seconds to look at the prompt card, an example of which is below, and then about two minutes to discuss the scenario with your partner. After that the examiner will ask you more questions related to the topic.

For **two** or **three** candidates

Scenario

> I'm going to describe a situation.
>
> **Your company is holding its annual seminar for all the sales representatives, and you are in charge of preparing the meeting room. Talk together for about two minutes about things you should provide and decide which three things are the most important.**
>
> Here are some ideas to help you.

Prompt material

ANNUAL SEMINAR

Mr A Smith

Follow-on questions

- Do you think annual meetings for staff are useful? (Why/Why not?)

- What makes a meeting successful? (Why?)

- What should the person who chairs a meeting do if some participants arrive late? (Why?)

- Do you say a lot at meetings? (Why/Why not?)

- Apart from meetings, in what other ways can companies communicate with their staff? (Why?)

Test 2

READING AND WRITING   1 hour 30 minutes

READING

PART ONE

Questions 1–5

- Look at questions **1–5**.
- In each question, which sentence is correct?
- For each question, mark one letter (**A**, **B** or **C**) on your Answer Sheet.

Example: 0

> *Don't forget –*
>
> *flight BA692   6.45 pm*

The plane arrives at

A   quarter to seven in the morning.
B   quarter past six in the evening.
C   quarter to seven in the evening.

The correct answer is **C**, so mark your Answer Sheet like this:

0	A	B	C
	☐	☐	▬

1

Customer Notice

We can supply three-drawer filing cabinets immediately, but two-drawer models are currently on order.

A   We can no longer sell two-drawer filing cabinets.
B   Our supplier of filing cabinets has gone out of business.
C   We are not fully stocked with filing cabinets at present.

2

> ## ANNUAL DINNER
>
> **Staff:** free   **Guests:** £10 (max. 1 guest per employee)
>
> Limited places available – BOOK NOW!

Staff who wish to attend the dinner

A   are allowed to invite only one person each.
B   must book today if they want to invite a friend.
C   have to pay £10 each for themselves and their partner.

3

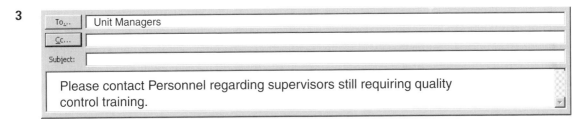

To...	Unit Managers
Cc...	
Subject:	

Please contact Personnel regarding supervisors still requiring quality control training.

Unit Managers should inform Personnel which staff

A   have received training.
B   are in need of training.
C   will supervise training.

4

> ## INTERNAL TELEPHONE DIRECTORY
> If any numbers need to be changed in this directory, please inform Extension 8286.

A   If you want information about numbers that have changed, contact Ext. 8286.
B   If any information in this directory is incorrect, contact Ext. 8286.
C   If you need a different directory, contact Ext. 8286.

5

> For economy reasons, employees travelling to the USA will fly overnight to Baltimore rather than Washington.

Employees flying to the USA will

A   no longer land in Washington.
B   arrive late at night.
C   be given economy class seats.

PART TWO

Questions 6–10

- Look at the list below. It shows the titles of chapters from a book about management.
- For questions **6–10**, decide which chapter (**A–H**) each person on the opposite page should read.
- For each question, mark one letter (**A–H**) on your Answer Sheet.
- Do not use any letter more than once.

THE MANAGER'S HANDBOOK

A Accounting: planning the advertising budget

B Finance: managing foreign exchange risks

C Personnel Management: creating productive work groups

D Information Management: sharing knowledge with employees

E Marketing: obtaining and using consumer information

F Production and Operations: managing the supply chain

G Global Communication: improving negotiation skills

H Project Management: ensuring research is well focused

6 Dominic works in international trade and needs to know how to finalise contracts with customers.

7 Sara is studying customer survey methods and needs to learn how to analyse the data.

8 Rachel works in an export department and wants information on how to avoid fluctuations in the value of export earnings.

9 Andreas wants to find out whether proposed changes to his company's promotion methods will result in necessary cost savings.

10 Alexander owns an advertising agency and wants to make better use of his staff's skills by organising them into effective teams.

PART THREE

Questions 11–15

- Look at the charts below. They show Internet sales compared to High Street sales of holidays offered by eight different travel companies during a three-year period.
- Which chart does each sentence (**11–15**) on the opposite page describe?
- For each sentence, mark one letter (**A–H**) on your Answer Sheet.
- Do not use any letter more than once.

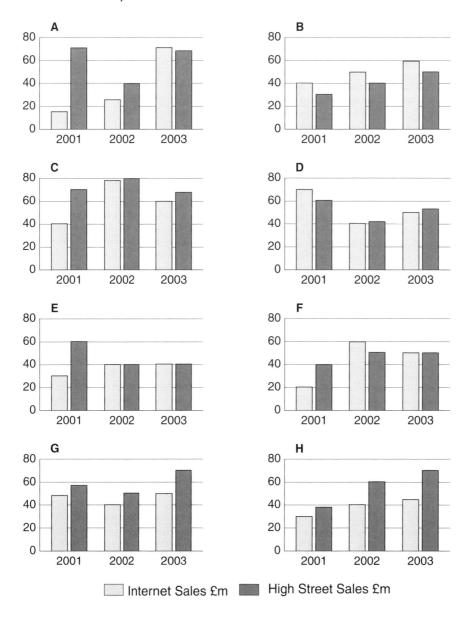

11   Although Internet sales started higher than High Street sales, they lost that lead when both dipped in the middle of the period.

12   High Street sales and Internet sales reached their peak in the middle of the period, but Internet sales declined more sharply at the end.

13   While both High Street and Internet sales rose throughout the period, High Street sales saw their greater increase in the middle year.

14   Both Internet and High Street sales dipped in the middle of the period, with the Internet always achieving fewer sales than the High Street.

15   High Street sales fell from their early high point to equal Internet sales, and both then remained level at the end of the period.

PART FOUR

Questions 16–22

- Read the article below about a hair products business.
- Are sentences **16–22** on the opposite page 'Right' or 'Wrong'? If there is not enough information to answer 'Right' or 'Wrong', choose 'Doesn't say'.
- For each sentence (**16–22**), mark one letter (**A, B** or **C**) on your Answer Sheet.

Louise Wood's Success Story

Three years ago, Louise Wood set up her own hair products company. She soon found she had more orders than she could handle by herself, and now employs ten people. Her turnover last year was £5.8 million.

'I used to work as a rep, selling hair products to people like famous hairdressers. One day someone suggested to me that I should make and sell similar products myself, and I thought, "Why not?"'

'Before I started, I thought running my own business would be similar to my previous job, but straight away I had problems I'd never dealt with before. I'm glad I took the risk, though.'

'I've always insisted on 90 days' credit to make the company self-supporting, without huge loans from banks. Luckily my manufacturers agreed!'

Louise uses local suppliers and expects them to come to her if they want to do business with her. 'I rarely leave the office and try to fit everything into normal working hours. I'm no good at working late.'

So what are Louise's plans now? 'My friends predicted I wouldn't keep this business for long as I'm always having new business ideas, but at the moment I want to see this project through.'

16 Louise Wood recruited her staff as soon as she set up her business.

   A Right   **B** Wrong   **C** Doesn't say

17 As a rep, Louise enjoyed meeting famous hairdressers.

   A Right   **B** Wrong   **C** Doesn't say

18 Louise's first few months of business were less difficult than she had expected.

   A Right   **B** Wrong   **C** Doesn't say

19 Louise has avoided borrowing large amounts of money to finance her business.

   A Right   **B** Wrong   **C** Doesn't say

20 Her suppliers have complained about having meetings at her office.

   A Right   **B** Wrong   **C** Doesn't say

21 Louise regularly does overtime.

   A Right   **B** Wrong   **C** Doesn't say

22 Louise feels committed to this business for the present.

   A Right   **B** Wrong   **C** Doesn't say

PART FIVE

Questions 23–28

- Read the text below, which is part of the annual report of a retail company called Bennetts. Its customers order goods from catalogues and collect them from the company's stores.
- For each question (**23–28**) on the opposite page, choose the correct answer.
- Mark one letter (**A**, **B** or **C**) on your Answer Sheet.

Chief Executive's Report

Bennetts has remained the region's leading catalogue retailer in the last twelve months. The company distributed around five million catalogues, a figure which is unchanged on the previous year, and we now have 98 stores, an increase of twelve. As was widely reported in the media, merger negotiations with another catalogue retailer ended without agreement.

It is true that this has been a difficult year, with a fall in trading profits, largely resulting from weaker consumer spending, but not helped by disappointing productivity levels in the stores. It is also a cause of worry that production costs are continuing to rise. However, changes in the way we deliver to stores have led to considerable savings.

With the aim of improving customer service and shopping convenience, we have introduced a number of new services in the last twelve months. Shopping by internet was added to the existing telephone ordering facility, and the early response to this has been good. In stores there are now information screens for customers to check the availability of goods they want to purchase. Together with other existing systems, which reduce queues and tell store customers when their orders are ready for collection, this is giving positive results.

Another change has been the replacement of the Traditional and Modern catalogues with a single catalogue. As a result, customers who used the Modern catalogue now have over 30% more products to choose from, although we have dropped the less popular lines. Annual printing costs already show the benefit of this move, and sales are expected to start growing within the next year.

We have had to change our plans for the coming year. It is clear that shoppers expect staff in stores to be both friendly and efficient. A major programme to raise standards will be introduced at once, while the planned improvements to store facilities will be delayed for twelve months. The proposed interactive TV shopping service will not now go ahead, and neither will the planned redevelopment of the corporate headquarters.

Bennetts is changing fast, and we are confident that the newly appointed members of the management team will help us to improve sales within the next twelve months, even if, as expected, there is no recovery in the economic climate. Our aim is to spend this time making sure that the company is as efficient as possible, and to delay our strategy of considering mergers or takeovers.

23   In the last year Bennetts has

   A   opened a number of new stores.
   B   merged with another catalogue company.
   C   increased the number of catalogues it delivers.

24   One improvement in the last year is that Bennetts has managed to

   A   spend less on manufacturing.
   B   increase productivity.
   C   reduce distribution costs.

25   As a result of developments in the last year, customers can now

   A   find out if goods are in stock before ordering them.
   B   collect their orders without queuing in the stores.
   C   order goods by telephone as well as in stores.

26   Replacing two catalogues with one has meant that

   A   all the lines from both catalogues are available.
   B   the catalogue has now become cheaper to produce.
   C   sales from the stores are already increasing.

27   Bennetts' main aim for next year is to improve

   A   home shopping facilities.
   B   the facilities at head office.
   C   customer service in the stores.

28   Bennetts is hopeful about the future because

   A   it expects the economic situation to improve.
   B   it has made changes to its management team.
   C   it is planning to take over other companies.

PART SIX

Questions 29–40

- Read the article below about attending job interviews.
- Choose the correct word to fill each gap, from **A**, **B** or **C** on the opposite page.
- For each question (**29–40**), mark one letter (**A, B** or **C**) on your Answer Sheet.

HOW TO SUCCEED AT INTERVIEWS

Preparation for interviews is essential. Interviewers like to see people that (**29**) .... prepared to ask questions about the company. (**30**) .... good interviewer is going to be looking for candidates (**31**) .... demonstrate that they will (**32**) .... something new to the company. Think of the things you (**33**) .... contribute to the organisation.

Looking good is also very important. (**34**) .... many companies now allow (**35**) .... formal clothes in the workplace, this does not mean it is no (**36**) .... essential to wear a suit for an interview. The most important thing is to be yourself. (**37**) .... you must never do is (**38**) .... to be something you are not, in order to get the job. If you have to do (**39**) ...., then you will probably not enjoy working in the position, (**40**) .... will the job be suitable for you.

29	**A**	be	**B**	are	**C**	is
30	**A**	Any	**B**	That	**C**	Some
31	**A**	which	**B**	whose	**C**	who
32	**A**	fetch	**B**	carry	**C**	bring
33	**A**	need	**B**	ought	**C**	could
34	**A**	Despite	**B**	Although	**C**	But
35	**A**	least	**B**	little	**C**	less
36	**A**	longer	**B**	further	**C**	more
37	**A**	What	**B**	How	**C**	Why
38	**A**	try	**B**	tried	**C**	tries
39	**A**	these	**B**	this	**C**	one
40	**A**	nor	**B**	not	**C**	never

PART SEVEN

Questions 41–45

- Read the email and the website page below.
- Complete the form on the opposite page.
- Write a word or phrase (in CAPITAL LETTERS) or a number on lines **41–45** on your Answer Sheet.

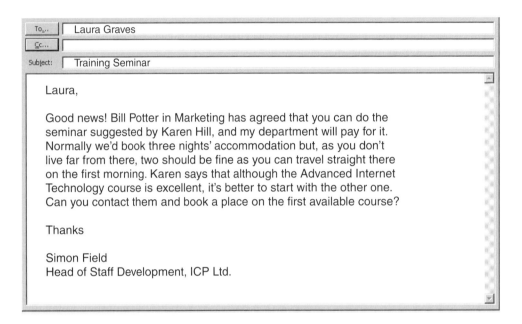

To...	Laura Graves
Cc...	
Subject:	Training Seminar

Laura,

Good news! Bill Potter in Marketing has agreed that you can do the seminar suggested by Karen Hill, and my department will pay for it. Normally we'd book three nights' accommodation but, as you don't live far from there, two should be fine as you can travel straight there on the first morning. Karen says that although the Advanced Internet Technology course is excellent, it's better to start with the other one. Can you contact them and book a place on the first available course?

Thanks

Simon Field
Head of Staff Development, ICP Ltd.

www.network.org

INTRODUCTORY AND DEVELOPMENT SEMINARS:

Date	Course	Places available
January 7–9	Advanced Internet Technology	6
January 11–13	Internet Strategies	0
January 14–16	Internet Strategies	2
Fees for each seminar:		

Seminar only (no accommodation)	Seminar + 2 nights' accommodation	Seminar + 3 nights' accommodation
£495	£655	£725

Network Seminars

ONLINE BOOKING FORM

FULL NAME OF PARTICIPANT: **(41)** ....

NAME OF COMPANY: I C P

DEPARTMENT TO INVOICE: **(42)** ....

TOTAL FEES PAYABLE: **(43)** £ ....

NAME OF PERSON WHO
RECOMMENDED THE COURSE: **(44)** ....

COURSE TITLE: **(45)** ....

WRITING

PART ONE

Question 46

- Your company has received a telephone complaint about late deliveries.
- Write a **note** to the Customer Services Manager in your company:
  - saying who has made the complaint
  - explaining why the deliveries were late
  - recommending what action should be taken.
- Write **30–40** words on your Answer Sheet.

PART TWO

Question 47

- You work for an advertising agency.
- Read the part of a letter below from a client, Ms Reeves, asking you to give a presentation to her colleagues.

> My colleagues would like to hear more about the new advertising campaign you are planning for our company and hope you will be able to give a short presentation at our department meeting on 15th December.
>
> I would be grateful if you would let me know as soon as you can whether this will be possible.

- Write a **letter** to Ms Reeves:
  - apologising for being unable to attend the meeting
  - explaining why you cannot attend
  - suggesting another date
  - asking her to contact your secretary to confirm the arrangements.
- Write **60–80** words on your Answer Sheet.
- Do not include any postal addresses.

LISTENING Approximately 40 minutes (including 10 minutes' transfer time)

LISTENING

PART ONE

Questions 1–8

- For questions **1–8** you will hear eight short recordings.
- For each question, mark **one** letter (**A**, **B** or **C**) for the correct answer.

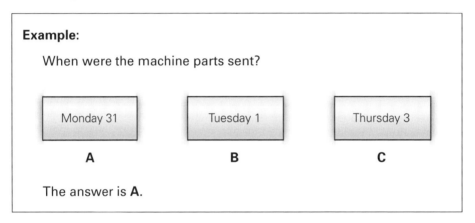

Example:

When were the machine parts sent?

Monday 31	Tuesday 1	Thursday 3
A	**B**	**C**

The answer is **A**.

- After you have listened once, replay each recording.

1 Why is the man late for the meeting?

    A   The meeting time was changed.
    B   His train was delayed.
    C   There was an emergency in his office.

2 Why is Timtex performing badly?

    A   Its profit margins are too narrow.
    B   It is targeting the wrong market.
    C   Demand for expensive clothing is low.

3 Which graph shows the company's sales?

A

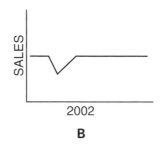

B

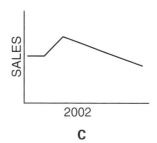

C

4 Where do they decide to hold the seminar?

A   at a conference centre
B   at a Trade Club
C   at a hotel

5 What does the successful business produce?

A

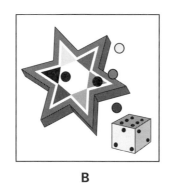

B

C

6 In which department does Ben work now?

A   Engineering
B   Sales
C   Marketing

7 Which chart shows the bank's current network of branches?

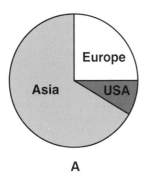

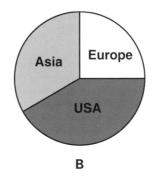

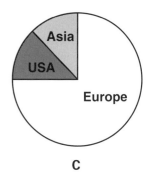

A

B

C

8 What do they still need to put in the hall?

A

B

C

PART TWO

Questions 9–15

- Look at the form below.
- Some information is missing.
- You will hear a woman booking exhibition space on the phone.
- For each question (**9–15**), fill in the missing information in the numbered space using a **word**, **numbers** or **letters**.
- After you have listened once, replay the recording.

Trade Fair Booking – June 2003

SPACE BOOKED: (9) .... sq m

COST: (10) £ ....

**ESTIMATED NUMBER OF PEOPLE
EXPECTED:** (11) ....

NAME OF CONFERENCE ROOM: (12) ....

SEATING CAPACITY: (13) ....

START TIME FOR ROOM: (14) ....

MAIN BOOKING REFERENCE: (15) ....

PART THREE

Questions 16–22

- Look at the notes below.
- Some information is missing.
- You will hear part of a talk given to a group of new employees.
- For each question (**16–22**), fill in the missing information in the numbered space using **one** or **two** words.
- After you have listened once, replay the recording.

First Day at NYP: Introduction

our Personnel Officer is: (16) Sarah ....

location of coffee
machines, noticeboards: (17) on ....

tax enquiries to: (18) ....

presentation: 3.30 pm

venue: Conference Room

subject: (19) ....

day of buffet lunch: (20) ....

for colour photocopiers
obtain: (21) ....

sports club – see Max
Collins for: (22) ....

PART FOUR

Questions 23–30

- You will hear a conversation between two senior managers of a large company based in the UK. They are talking about a visit to the company by a group of foreign executives.
- For each question (**23–30**), mark **one** letter (**A**, **B** or **C**) for the correct answer.
- After you have listened once, replay the recording.

23 When will the visitors arrive?

    A   March
    B   April
    C   May

24 How many visitors are coming?

    A   six
    B   seven
    C   eight

25 What will the visitors see on the first day?

    A   the retail outlets
    B   the factory in Swindon
    C   the company headquarters

26 What are the visitors *most* interested in?

    A   company performance
    B   new technology
    C   working practices

27 Who do the visitors particularly want to meet?

    A   the Human Resources group
    B   the Board of Directors
    C   the Customer Services team

28   What will the presentation be about?

    A   rewards for employees
    B   company organisation
    C   negotiating techniques

29   What will the group do in London?

    A   visit a new commercial building
    B   go to an official reception
    C   meet some important politicians

30   Where will the visitors go on the final day?

    A   to an exhibition centre in Birmingham
    B   to a factory in the North East
    C   to several sites in Scotland

You now have 10 minutes to transfer your answers to your Answer Sheet.

SPEAKING   12 minutes

SAMPLE SPEAKING TASKS

PART ONE

The interview – about 2 minutes

In this part the interlocutor asks questions to each of the candidates in turn. You have to give information about yourself and express personal opinions.

PART TWO

'Mini presentation' – about 5 minutes

In this part of the test you are asked to give a short talk on a business topic. You have to choose one of the topics from the two below and then talk for about one minute. You have one minute to prepare your ideas.

A   WHAT IS IMPORTANT WHEN . . .?

CHOOSING A PART-TIME JOB

- WORKING HOURS
- RESPONSIBILITIES
- PAY

B   WHAT IS IMPORTANT WHEN . . .?

DECIDING TO ATTEND A CONFERENCE

- TOPICS
- VENUE
- COST

PART THREE

Discussion – about 5 minutes

In this part of the test the examiner reads out a scenario and gives you some prompt material in the form of pictures or words. You have 30 seconds to look at the prompt card, an example of which is below, and then about two minutes to discuss the scenario with your partner. After that the examiner will ask you more questions related to the topic.

For **two** or **three** candidates

Scenario

I'm going to describe a situation.

Your company has performed very well this year, and managers want to thank all the staff. Talk together for about two minutes about ways of rewarding staff and decide which one is the best.

Here are some ideas to help you.

Prompt material

Rewards for staff

- bonus payment
- party
- day trip
- gift
- shares in the company
- extra day's holiday

Follow-on questions

- Is there any other reward you would like? (Why?)

- Is it important for all staff to receive the same type of reward? (Why/Why not?)

- What kind of place would be suitable for a company trip? (Why?)

- How important is it to reward staff for good work? (Why?)

- Should companies have a regular programme of social events for staff? (Why/Why not?)

Test 3

READING AND WRITING   1 hour 30 minutes

READING

PART ONE

Questions 1–5

- Look at questions **1–5**.
- In each question, which sentence is correct?
- For each question, mark one letter (**A**, **B** or **C**) on your Answer Sheet.

Example: 0

Telephone message

Bill Ryan caught 9.30 flight – due here
11.30 now, not 12.30

When does Bill Ryan expect to arrive?

A   9.30
B   11.30
C   12.30

The correct answer is **B**, so mark your Answer Sheet like this:

0	A	B	C
	▭	▬	▭

1

> **Looking for a top job? Contact Jobservices.com
> for a better presented CV**

A   Jobservices.com will find you a better job, depending on your CV.
B   Improve the look of your CV with the help of Jobservices.com.
C   If your CV is well presented, Jobservices.com will employ you.

2

> All prices shown are inclusive of any promotional
> offer and tax at the current rate.

A   The price on the item is the final selling price.
B   Tax will be added to the item price at point of sale.
C   The current promotional offer is free of tax.

3

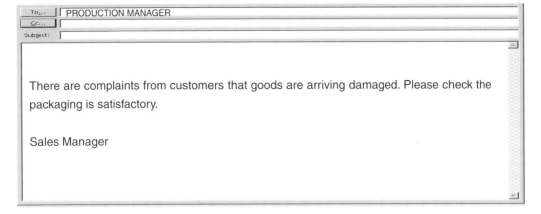

To... PRODUCTION MANAGER
Cc...
Subject:

There are complaints from customers that goods are arriving damaged. Please check the packaging is satisfactory.

Sales Manager

The Production Manager must find out

A who is packing the goods.
B which goods are damaged.
C how the goods are packed.

4

FINANCE DEPARTMENT RELOCATION

Friday's meeting is compulsory for all Finance staff;
others welcome to attend for information.

A The meeting is about something which affects only one department.
B Staff in all departments should attend the meeting.
C Finance will announce at the meeting which departments will relocate.

5

Accounts clerk wanted

**£12,000 per year. Experience an
advantage. Full training provided.
Immediate availability essential.
Call 01636-619432 now.**

Applicants for the above post

A need previous experience of this work.
B should be qualified already in this work.
C must be able to start work straightaway.

PART TWO

Questions 6–10

- Look at the list below. It shows a number of tasks that staff need to do in order to organise an anniversary party for their company.
- For questions **6–10**, decide which task (**A–H**) would be most suitable for each person on the opposite page.
- For each question, mark the correct letter (**A–H**) on your Answer Sheet.
- Do not use any letter more than once.

~ Anniversary Party ~

A Find suitable place to hold party

B Organise food and drinks (catering specialist needed)

C Create attractive invitations and posters

D Find guest speaker – e.g. a local business leader good at public speaking

E Type address labels for invitations

F Book local hotel accommodation for guests

G Select and check availability of entertainers

H Meet and greet guests on arrival (confident person required)

6 Andrew Taylor used to work for a PR company, so has good social skills and mixes well at public events.

7 Robin Richards is skilled in art and computer-aided design, and previously worked for a publicity company.

8 Fiona Murphy used to work for a local business producing CDs and has contacts with performers in the music business.

9 Since working as an office manager, Mary Smith has gained experience of booking large local venues for entertainment events.

10 John Albright, who worked briefly as a hotel porter, has developed accurate keyboard skills since he joined the company.

PART THREE

Questions 11–15

- Look at the table and charts below. They show the market share, annual turnover and share prices for eight electronics manufacturing companies between 1999 and 2002.
- Which company does each sentence (**11–15**) describe?
- For each sentence, mark one letter (**A–H**) on your Answer Sheet.
- Do not use any letter more than once.

MARKET SHARE (%)

COMPANY	1999	2002
A	5	7
B	9	15
C	32	39
D	15	9
E	10	10
F	17	8
G	3	5
H	9	7

TURNOVER (£ MILLION)

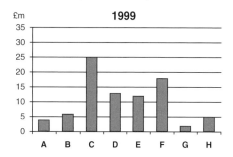

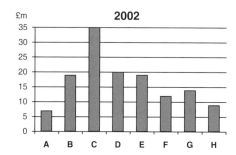

MAXIMUM AND MINIMUM SHARE PRICES (£) 1999–2002

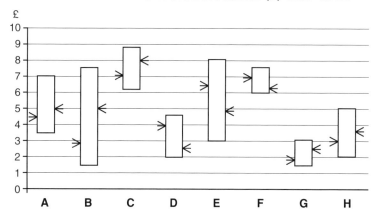

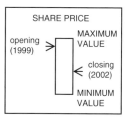

11   This company's share price ended the period lower than it started, its market share declined sharply, and its turnover also dropped.

12   Although this company's market share declined over the period, its turnover almost doubled and the share price closed higher than it opened.

13   Despite increasing its turnover, this company was unable to keep its strong market share, which, like its share price, ended below its 1999 level.

14   Shares in this company ended the period close to matching their best performance, while market share and turnover rose from already strong positions.

15   While this company's market share and turnover increased slightly from low levels, its share price closed well below its maximum value of the period.

PART FOUR

Questions 16–22

- Read the newspaper article below about moving premises.
- Are sentences **16–22** on the opposite page 'Right' or 'Wrong'? If there is not enough information to answer 'Right' or 'Wrong', choose 'Doesn't say'.
- For each sentence (**16–22**), mark one letter (**A**, **B** or **C**) on your Answer Sheet.

How to move office

A successful office relocation demands careful preparation. It's important to form a project team as early as possible before the move, and at least twelve months in advance. It's also essential to contact the British Association of Removers and ask for a list of commercial specialists who will advise on packing, security and other important topics.

Internally you'll need to appoint a move organiser, or employ a freelance expert from a firm such as Move Plan, which organises relocation for firms from two to 6,000 people. You'll also need to pick a time when closing down your IT department will cause the fewest problems to the business and, for that reason, the majority of firms now move over a weekend.

Next make a list of all the furniture, equipment and paperwork. Commercial movers will pack filing in A–Z order, so if A–G leaves the building, it's still A–G when it's unpacked. Confidential files can be sealed in secure boxes for the moving day.

Commercial specialists will keep company employees fully informed and answer any questions they may have. You may move offices once or twice in your career, but experts do it every day.

16 According to the article, the minimum planning time for an office move should be a year.

A Right   **B** Wrong   **C** Doesn't say

17 The writer says that companies should be able to organise their move without external help.

A Right   **B** Wrong   **C** Doesn't say

18 Move Plan are experts at organising both large and small moves.

A Right   **B** Wrong   **C** Doesn't say

19 The IT department is usually the first department to move.

A Right   **B** Wrong   **C** Doesn't say

20 Most companies believe there are fewer computer problems if the move happens Monday to Friday.

A Right   **B** Wrong   **C** Doesn't say

21 Companies are advised to pack confidential materials themselves.

A Right   **B** Wrong   **C** Doesn't say

22 A specialist remover will make sure staff are kept up to date with arrangements for their move.

A Right   **B** Wrong   **C** Doesn't say

PART FIVE

Questions 23–28

- Read the newspaper article below about Sandersley, a British company which organises package holidays abroad.
- For each question (**23–28**), on the opposite page, choose the correct answer.
- Mark one letter (**A**, **B** or **C**) on your Answer Sheet.

Package Holiday Success

Travel operator Sandersley is different from most of its rivals. UK package holiday companies would love to have plenty of repeat business. Instead, in an effort to attract trade, they are forced to spend enormous sums on marketing – but they are operating in a very competitive market. So, although the big travel companies try hard to create attractive brands, if you ask the customers delayed at airports, many aren't even sure which company they've booked with. Ask customers of Sandersley, however, and this is probably their third or fourth holiday with the company.

A Sandersley holiday doesn't come cheap; but for their customers this isn't an issue. The attraction is that they get an activity-based 'club' which has escaped the notice of the general public. Even the location of the holiday is of minor importance.

A high proportion of customers are families, because the adults are free to enjoy the activities on offer, while small children are in the care of people employed by Sandersley just for this purpose. These nannies get free flights and meals on top of their pay.

Interestingly, most of the company's senior managers began at the bottom: for example, Carol Fletcher, the Marketing Manager, came as a ski guide in 1985, went away to set up her own catering business, sold it for a considerable sum, and returned to Sandersley in the late 1990s.

The company's performance over the years means that it gets a steady stream of offers from large tour operators wanting to buy the company. Jerry Baker, who started the firm, came very close to selling

it for £30 million a few years ago. But at the last minute, Garmond, the potential buyer, was itself taken over by an American travel company which didn't see a place for Sandersley in the group.

So where does that leave Sandersley? Despite greatly increasing its turnover in the past four years, the company has a careful attitude to expansion. Its decision not to sell skiing holidays in North America proved the right one when many of its rivals failed to persuade British travellers to take the ten-hour flight. Learning from experiences like these, Sandersley's two recent departures from its main activity are the acquisitions of restaurant chains in Spain and in Turkey. And as for moving into the mass market for its holidays? Sandersley is much too successful to want to do that.

23   Sandersley differs from most other UK travel operators in

    A   the cost of its holidays.
    B   the places where it advertises.
    C   the number of repeat bookings it has.

24   Sandersley's customers like

    A   the places where the company organises holidays.
    B   the fact that the company is not well known.
    C   the prices that the company charges for its holidays.

25   The company attracts families because

    A   it arranges joint activities for adults and children.
    B   it has staff who look after children.
    C   it provides free holidays for children.

26   In what way is Carol Fletcher typical of the company's senior staff?

    A   She started working for the company at a low level.
    B   She brought experience from another industry.
    C   She used to run her own company.

27   Sandersley was not sold because

    A   Garmond believed the price was too high.
    B   Garmond's new owner decided against the purchase.
    C   Garmond felt unhappy with Sandersley's performance.

28   What is Sandersley's strategy for expansion?

    A   to offer holidays in different countries
    B   to increase the customer base for its holidays
    C   to depend less on the holiday industry

PART SIX

Questions 29–40

- Read the newspaper report below about working in sales.
- Choose the correct word to fill each gap, from **A**, **B** or **C** on the opposite page.
- For each question (**29–40**), mark one letter (**A**, **B** or **C**) on your Answer Sheet.

WORKING IN SALES

Working in sales is one of the few areas where first impressions really matter. Good sales people (**29**) .... to have the personality to get on with customers. Three years ago, Julian Agostino identified a (**30**) .... for matching (**31**) .... right people to sales jobs, and began Sales Moves, a recruitment fair, to achieve (**32**) .... He got the idea after he was (**33**) .... in setting up a telesales company and found (**34**) .... was difficult to recruit good people. He says:

'(**35**) .... the sales sector is enormous, there appeared to be (**36**) .... specialist recruitment help. I decided to hold fairs across the country, which allowed employers and employees to meet.' His company is doing very well. (**37**) .... recently, most companies asked for graduates and offered the chance to go on to work in (**38**) .... parts of the company later on. Today, many are more interested (**39**) .... recruiting good sales people – high achievers (**40**) .... career will continue in sales.

29	**A**	need	**B**	must	**C**	should
30	**A**	request	**B**	claim	**C**	demand
31	**A**	a	**B**	some	**C**	the
32	**A**	there	**B**	this	**C**	those
33	**A**	involved	**B**	concerned	**C**	required
34	**A**	that	**B**	it	**C**	he
35	**A**	Although	**B**	Despite	**C**	If
36	**A**	any	**B**	few	**C**	no
37	**A**	Now	**B**	After	**C**	Until
38	**A**	other	**B**	another	**C**	others
39	**A**	on	**B**	in	**C**	at
40	**A**	who	**B**	which	**C**	whose

PART SEVEN

Questions 41–45

- Read the memo and the advertisement below.
- Complete the form on the opposite page.
- Write a word or phrase (in CAPITAL LETTERS) or a number on lines **41–45** on your Answer Sheet.

EAP Ltd
MEMO

To:	**Paula Smith**
From:	**Alan Blackman**
Date:	**24 May 2003**
Subject:	**Website Company**

I think this website company would help our business. Could you fill in the form and ask for further details? Put me down as the contact person (they can email me). I think we'd like to start with a couple of photos and whatever their minimum number of pages is. We'll need to change details every month, I expect.

---

102 • Computer Today Magazine

OnNet – Business Websites

Will a website work for you?

The answer is YES!

Standard rates	
Website design:	$75 per page (3 page minimum) $5 to $10 per photo
Website hosting:	$20 per month

Update your website daily, weekly or monthly.

Contact: sales@onnet.com
Tel: 10177834-436
Fax: 10178652-768

✂ -

OnNet

Company: EAP Ltd

Contact person (full name):   **(41)** ....

Number of pages: **(42)** .... pages

Number of photos: 2 photos

How often will you want to update   **(43)** ....
your website?

How would you like us to contact   **(44)** ....
you?

Where did you see our advert?   **(45)** in ....

WRITING

PART ONE

Question 46

- You have recently started a new job and the Personnel Manager has asked you to write an article for the company magazine.
- Write a **note** to the Personnel Manager:
  - agreeing to write the article
  - giving brief details of what you will write about
  - asking about the deadline for the article.
- Write **30–40** words on your Answer Sheet.

> To: Bill Evans, Personnel Manager
>
> ....
>
> ....
>
> ....
>
> ....
>
> ....
>
> ....

PART TWO

Question 47

● Read the part of a letter below from Mr Hutton, the manager of an office supplies company.

> You haven't placed an order with our company for 6 months. I am worried that we have not heard from you. We will be happy to agree a small discount on your next order of office supplies.
>
> If there is any problem, please contact me and I'll be happy to help.

● Write a **letter** to Mr Hutton:
  ● thanking him for the letter
  ● explaining why you were unhappy with the last delivery of his products
  ● requesting an up-to-date catalogue
  ● saying how much discount you want.
● Write **60–80** words on your Answer Sheet.
● Do not include any postal addresses.

LISTENING   Approximately 40 minutes (including 10 minutes' transfer time)

LISTENING

PART ONE

Questions 1–8

- For questions **1–8** you will hear eight short recordings.
- For each question, mark **one** letter (**A**, **B** or **C**) for the correct answer.

Example:

Who is Emily going to write to?

A the staff
B the supplier
C the clients

The answer is **A**.

- After you have listened once, replay each recording.

1 Who does the man need to speak to?

A Charles Pearson
B John Vernon
C Peter Tribe

2 Where is the man telephoning from?

A his office
B his hotel
C his home

3   How many job applications have they received in total?

100	300	500
A	**B**	**C**

4   How will the company carry out their market research?

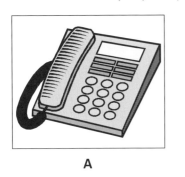

A

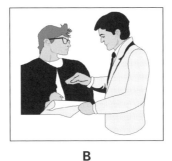

B

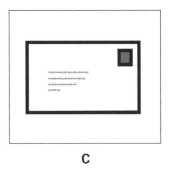

C

5   Which graph is correct?

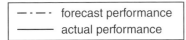

— · — forecast performance
—— actual performance

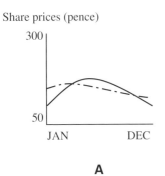

A

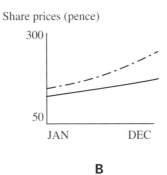

B

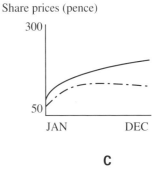

C

6 When is the woman going to take her holiday?

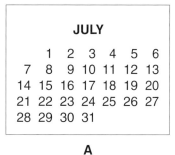

JULY	AUGUST	SEPTEMBER
A	B	C

7 What was the man's opinion of the presentation?

A He thought it was good.
B He was bored.
C He found it confusing.

8 Which chart shows the company's turnover?

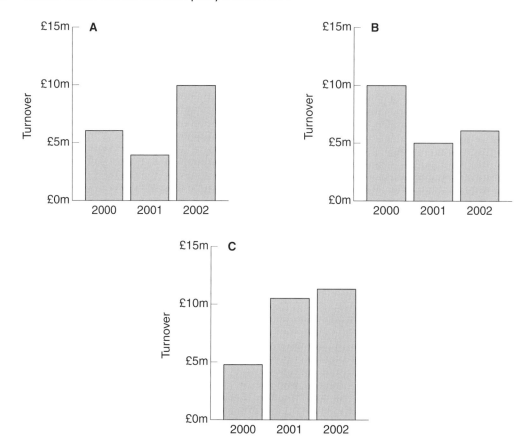

PART TWO

Questions 9–15

- Look at the form below.
- Some information is missing.
- You will hear a man discussing an order for some factory equipment.
- For each question (**9–15**), fill in the missing information in the numbered space using a **word**, **numbers** or **letters**.
- After you have listened once, replay the recording.

Changes to Order

CUSTOMER:	Amstel Machine Tools
PRODUCT:	Workshop tables
ORDER REFERENCE NUMBER:	(9) ....
NEW SIZE REQUIRED	
WIDTH:	(10) .... cm
LENGTH:	212 cm
HEIGHT:	(11) .... cm
QUANTITY:	(12) ....
PRICE PER ITEM:	(13) £ ....
NEW DISCOUNT:	(14) .... %
CONTACT NAME:	(15) Paul ....

PART THREE

Questions 16–22

- Look at the notes below about a chain of department stores.
- Some information is missing.
- You will hear part of a talk given by the company's Human Resources manager.
- For each question (**16–22**), fill in the missing information in the numbered space using **one** or **two** words.
- After you have listened once, replay the recording.

Dennings

Dennings Retail Group
Famous for selling: (16) ....

25 UK stores. Location
of newest store in UK: (17) ....

4 stores abroad. Next
store to open abroad: (18) ....

New project (Dennings
Internet Shopping) starts: (19) 2004

Employment at Dennings
High salaries

All staff can belong to   (20) .... scheme

Currently recruiting staff
for the   (21) .... course

Run special introduction
week for   (22) ....

PART FOUR

Questions 23–30

- You will hear a radio interview. The interviewer is talking to a young businessman called James Osmond, who publishes a successful magazine called *Day by Day*.
- For each question (**23–30**), mark **one** letter (**A**, **B** or **C**) for the correct answer.
- After you have listened once, replay the recording.

23 How long has the magazine been on sale?

A for one year
B for eighteen months
C for two years

24 Where did James Osmond work before he started the magazine?

A on a newspaper
B in the travel business
C at a bank

25 Who helped James Osmond to plan the magazine?

A a magazine editor
B a publishing company
C a company director

26 What is the main topic of James Osmond's magazine?

A careers
B health
C leisure

27 Which kind of people does James Osmond prefer to work with?

A friends and family
B famous people
C professionals

28 Who provides the extra financing the magazine needs now?

  A several banks
  B private individuals
  C an investment company

29 What does James Osmond say about current sales of the magazine?

  A They have increased every month.
  B They have levelled off.
  C They have begun to fall slightly.

30 How does James Osmond plan to develop the magazine next year?

  A by changing its design
  B by advertising it more widely
  C by expanding its distribution

You now have 10 minutes to transfer your answers to your Answer Sheet.

SPEAKING   12 minutes

SAMPLE SPEAKING TASKS

PART ONE

The interview – about 2 minutes

In this part the interlocutor asks questions to each of the candidates in turn. You have to give information about yourself and express personal opinions.

PART TWO

'Mini presentation' – about 5 minutes

In this part of the test you are asked to give a short talk on a business topic. You have to choose one of the topics from the two below and then talk for about one minute. You have one minute to prepare your ideas.

A   WHAT IS IMPORTANT WHEN . . .?

LOOKING FOR A NEW JOB

- CAREER OPPORTUNITIES
- LOCATION OF JOB
- POSSIBILITY OF MAKING BUSINESS TRIPS

B   WHAT IS IMPORTANT WHEN . . .?

TRAVELLING BY AIR FOR BUSINESS

- FLIGHT DEPARTURE TIMES
- IN-FLIGHT SERVICE
- TRANSPORT TO AND FROM AIRPORTS

PART THREE

Discussion – about 5 minutes

In this part of the test the examiner reads out a scenario and gives you some prompt material in the form of pictures or words. You have 30 seconds to look at the prompt card, an example of which is below, and then about two minutes to discuss the scenario with your partner. After that the examiner will ask you more questions related to the topic.

For **two** or **three** candidates

Scenario

> I'm going to describe a situation.
>
> **A large retail company is choosing some gifts to help promote the company. Talk together for about two minutes about the possible gifts and decide which three gifts would be most suitable.**
>
> Here are some ideas to help you.

Prompt material

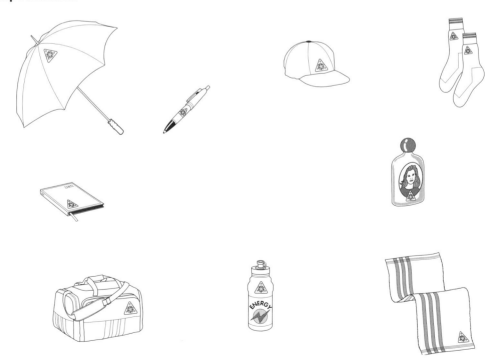

Follow-on questions

- What kind of gift would you find the most useful? (Why?)
- Do you think promotional gifts should be expensive? (Why/Why not?)
- Who should companies give promotional gifts to? (Why?)
- Why is it important for companies to give gifts to their clients?
- What other ways are there to promote a company?

Test 4

READING AND WRITING   1 hour 30 minutes

READING

PART ONE

Questions 1–5

- Look at questions **1–5**.
- In each question, which sentence is correct?
- For each question, mark one letter (**A**, **B** or **C**) on your Answer Sheet.

Example: 0

Telephone message

Bill Ryan caught 9.30 flight – due here
11.30 now, not 12.30

When does Bill Ryan expect to arrive?

A   9.30
B   11.30
C   12.30

The correct answer is **B**, so mark your Answer Sheet like this:

0	A	B	C
	▭	▬	▭

1

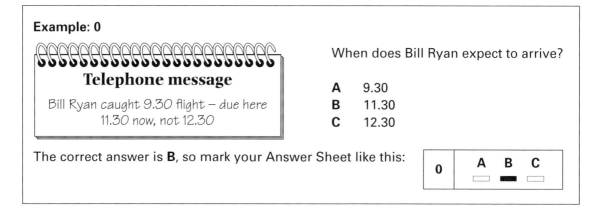

To... | All Staff
Cc... |
Subject: | Staff Changes

From July Tony Barnes from Sales will work in Marketing to replace Jane Crew, who moves to Administration.

In which department is Jane Crew working at the moment?

A   Sales
B   Marketing
C   Administration

2

> **Special Offer! Limited period only.**
> **0% commission on foreign currency exchange.**

A Commission is charged on some foreign currencies only.

B Customers can change limited amounts of money without paying commission.

C At present there is no charge for changing foreign money.

3

> To receive our free business publications, complete and return the enclosed form – up to three titles per company.

A Each company may send for three publications.

B Companies may send in three articles for publication.

C Publications are sent out on receipt of payment and form.

4

> **Business Latest**
>
> **Demand for office space in sharp decline due to a slowing economy.**
>
> Click here

A Companies may have to wait longer to find cheap offices to rent.

B The financial situation is affecting the commercial property market.

C Businesses are renting out empty office space to help their falling profits.

5

> **Office furniture direct from the manufacturer**
> **Free delivery; 21-day money back trial; interest free credit;**
> **2-year guarantee**

A Buyers will get a full refund if they are not satisfied.

B Customers must collect the furniture straight from the factory.

C Payment for the furniture has to be completed within two years.

PART TWO

Questions 6–10

- Look at the contents page below. It shows the titles of eight different sections of a business directory.
- For questions **6–10**, decide which section of the directory (**A–H**) each person on the opposite page should look at.
- For each question, mark one letter (**A–H**) on your Answer Sheet.
- Do not use any letter more than once.

Contents

A Computer Printers – service and repairs

B Computer Systems and Software – sales

C Computer Training Services

D Corporate Entertainment Providers

E Courier Services

F Employment and Recruitment Agencies

G Exhibition and Trade Fair Organisers – national and international

H Office Furniture

6 Sally's MD wants to reorganise the office because of a new computer system, so Sally is researching computer desks for him.

7 Frank wants to involve recruits to his website company in a day of social activities in order to encourage team-building.

8 Alexandra runs a successful international translation agency and she thinks her computers need upgrading because her database is now so large.

9 David has received some brochures from the printers and he needs to get them delivered to an exhibition centre quickly.

10 Sue is setting up a company magazine and wants all the new staff involved to become skilled at desktop publishing.

PART THREE

Questions 11–15

- Look at the charts below. They show profits before tax and profit margins for eight different companies from 1998 to 2002.
- Which chart does each sentence (**11–15**) describe?
- For each sentence, mark one letter (**A–H**) on your Answer Sheet.
- Do not use any letter more than once.

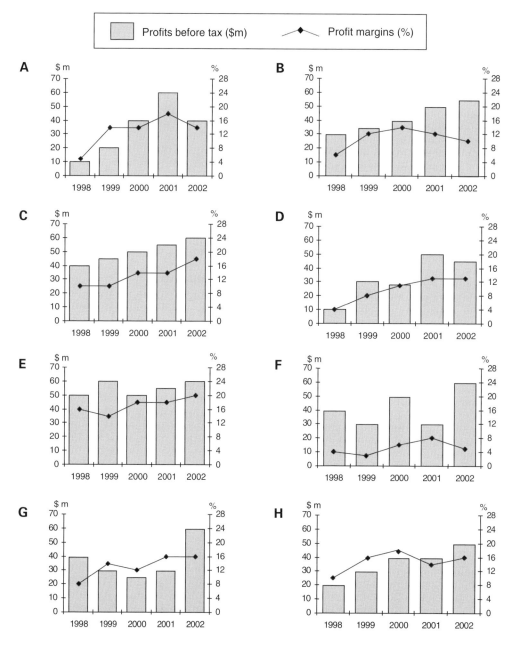

11 The company's profit margins have decreased over the most recent years, while profits before tax have maintained a steady rise since 1998.

12 In 2002 the company both regained its 1999 level of profits before tax and also managed to improve profit margins.

13 2002 saw a great improvement in profits before tax but the company's profit margins remained unchanged at the end of the period.

14 The last five years have seen alternate rises and falls in profits before tax, at the same time as fluctuating profit margins for the company.

15 Even though the company reached record levels of both profits before tax and profit margins in 2001, neither of these was maintained.

PART FOUR

Questions 16–22

- Read the newspaper article below about a retail company's performance.
- Are sentences **16–22** on the opposite page 'Right' or 'Wrong'? If there is not enough information to answer 'Right' or 'Wrong', choose 'Doesn't say'.
- For each sentence (**16–22**), mark one letter (**A**, **B** or **C**) on your Answer Sheet.

SHAREHOLDERS WATCH HOCKING CLOSELY

Hocking, the High Street retailer, yesterday published figures indicating a recovery in sales for the first three months of the year; this pleased the company's shareholders, who have had a difficult time in recent years. The news was not all good, however. Sales at Hocking's sister company, Hocking's Pharmacy, were disappointing, improving by only 0.7 per cent during the period.

James Bowen, the company chairman, said, 'The retail climate is improving slowly. Our retail businesses found that trading conditions were reasonable in April, very poor in May, then improved considerably in June, with this improvement continuing in July. Operating costs are growing more slowly than sales, so our profit forecasts for the rest of the year are good.'

The company said that it will install customer computer kiosks in more than 250 stores by Christmas, after a trial period in 20 stores in the north of England saw sales rise by 5 per cent. These computer kiosks allow specially targeted discounts and promotions to be offered to individual customers.

16   Hocking, the retailer, has shown signs of improved sales in the first quarter of the year.

    A Right   **B** Wrong   **C** Doesn't say

17   The price of shares in Hocking, the retailer, has risen slightly.

    A Right   **B** Wrong   **C** Doesn't say

18   Sales figures at Hocking's Pharmacy showed a slight fall.

    A Right   **B** Wrong   **C** Doesn't say

19   According to the chairman, trading conditions have improved steadily each month since April.

    A Right   **B** Wrong   **C** Doesn't say

20   The chairman predicts an improvement in profits as sales are rising faster than operating costs.

    A Right   **B** Wrong   **C** Doesn't say

21   Hocking's computer kiosks have already shown that they can lead to increased sales.

    A Right   **B** Wrong   **C** Doesn't say

22   Customers asked for clearer information to be provided about discounts and promotions.

    A Right   **B** Wrong   **C** Doesn't say

PART FIVE

Questions 23–28

- Read the article below about Gordon Jackman, who runs a computer software company.
- For each question (**23–28**), on the opposite page, choose the correct answer.
- Mark one letter (**A**, **B** or **C**) on your Answer Sheet.

Software from the kitchen

If you want to know what someone is like, look at their office. Tidy desk, efficient mind. Untidy desk, busy mind. But this doesn't fit Gordon Jackman, who started business software producer Quillatic. He works at home, in the untidiest kitchen I've ever seen, yet he strangely hates untidiness in business more than anything else. At the same time he admits that he has little interest in detail.

Jackman describes his colleagues as 'sweepers'. He explains: 'I can only get as far as the first 80% of an idea, but I know this weakness, so I leave it to everyone else to finish my ideas, to make sure details aren't forgotten. People who don't know their weaknesses run untidy companies and have unhappy companies.'

Jackman is a strong believer in testing people's personal qualities as part of the recruitment process, and he and his 60 employees were all tested. He admits that such a strong belief in this is unusual in business, but adds, 'Have you ever noticed how teachers seem to be the same type of person? People do seem to select the job that's right for their type.'

Most of his ideas, he says, are not new but come from reading just about every management book that's published. 'You wouldn't expect a doctor not to have read anything about medicine since qualifying, yet with management it seems to be allowed,' he says. 'You have to read whatever's out there. Even if a book gives you only one idea, it's something you didn't have before.'

Jackman believes in developing his staff, but business deals come first. 'I believe in appointing people to do what they can and not more. So, for example, at the moment I have a very good salesman who has almost completed a sale but won't close the deal himself as he doesn't have enough experience yet.'

At the same time, he has strong ideas about rewards. 'Sales staff can earn as much as managers, because I recognise that if one person's doing a great job at managing, and another at selling, there's no reason for a difference in pay. And although experience may make a difference, in the end it's actions that count.'

Running a company from a kitchen may not be recommended by many writers on management, but for Gordon Jackman it's a great success.

23 In the first paragraph, the writer suggests that Gordon Jackman is

    A   unsuccessful in business.

    B   typical of computer experts.

    C   difficult to fully understand.

24 Jackman uses the word 'sweepers' to describe people who

    A   finish off things that someone else starts.

    B   start things but don't finish them.

    C   work with a project from beginning to end.

25 Jackman believes that

    A   companies need to employ people who are of a similar type.

    B   people usually look for jobs which suit the type of person they are.

    C   tests of personal qualities are taken too seriously by most companies.

26 Jackman believes that both business people and doctors

    A   have to be good at management.

    B   should keep up to date with their field.

    C   need to select reading material carefully.

27 What point does Jackman make about his staff?

    A   Employees should be trained to do particular jobs.

    B   Staff development matters less than the success of a deal.

    C   Teamwork is essential for carrying out all tasks.

28 Jackman pays staff according to

    A   how well they do their job.

    B   their position in the company.

    C   the amount of experience they have.

PART SIX

Questions 29–40

- Read the article below about a sportswear company.
- Choose the correct word to fill each gap, from **A**, **B** or **C** on the opposite page.
- For each question (**29–40**), mark one letter (**A**, **B** or **C**) on your Answer Sheet.

A success story

Tony Pearson was appointed to the board of *Greens*, the sportswear company, as Chief Executive nine months ago. He has (**29**) .... almost 27 years in clothes retailing, previously (**30**) .... a senior position with *Munroes*, a company with as (**31**) .... as 300 retail outlets across the UK.

Pearson is responsible for the company's latest five-year plan. His general strategy has been to increase profits by expanding *Greens'* product (**32**) ...., and so far the policy has worked. Stores (**33**) .... report a sales growth (**34**) .... about 20% this year.

A (**35**) .... 35 stores were redesigned in the current year (**36**) .... a cost of £23 million. In addition, ten new stores are expected to open (**37**) .... year for the next three or four years. Two of (**38**) .... new stores will be outside the UK. Mr Pearson says the company (**39**) .... intends to increase the (**40**) .... of distribution centres, and improve customer services.

Overall, Tony Pearson's business strategy seems to be proving very successful.

29	**A**	taken	**B**	passed	**C**	spent
30	**A**	held	**B**	holding	**C**	holds
31	**A**	much	**B**	most	**C**	many
32	**A**	variety	**B**	range	**C**	collection
33	**A**	have	**B**	should	**C**	ought
34	**A**	in	**B**	till	**C**	of
35	**A**	later	**B**	further	**C**	greater
36	**A**	at	**B**	from	**C**	by
37	**A**	another	**B**	any	**C**	each
38	**A**	these	**B**	they	**C**	them
39	**A**	ever	**B**	too	**C**	also
40	**A**	number	**B**	figure	**C**	sum

PART SEVEN

Questions 41–45

- Read the memo and advertisement below.
- Complete the form on the opposite page.
- Write a word or phrase (in CAPITAL LETTERS) or a number on lines **41–45** on your Answer Sheet.

Memo

To:	Paul Janner, Training Dept
From:	Simon Hastings, Sales
Date:	5 Oct 2003
Subject:	Language course

As my department has won some new business abroad, I need to improve my Spanish and German. I have enclosed an ad for a language organisation – my wife learnt Arabic with them very successfully. I can already speak some German – for ordinary conversation, anyway – so I'll start with a Business course in that, and leave Spanish till later. I'm not a beginner but I won't be good enough for the Advanced class.

Could you book a course for me ASAP, please, and arrange accommodation – I'd prefer not to stay with a family.

Otis Language Courses

- Learn Arabic in Cairo, German in Berlin or Spanish in Madrid
- Beginner, Intermediate and Advanced levels
- Choose a Conversation, an Examination or a Business course
- Accommodation in hotel or with host family

Otis Language Courses – BOOKING FORM

Full name of participant: **(41)** ....

Course language: **(42)** ....

Course focus: **(43)** ....

Level: **(44)** ....

Starting date: *ASAP*

Type of accommodation required: **(45)** ....

WRITING

PART ONE

Question 46

- Your work team is scheduled to complete a project next month, but there has been a delay.
- Write an **email** to the department manager:
  - apologising for the delay
  - giving the reason for the delay
  - saying what help you need to complete the project.
- Write **30–40** words on your Answer Sheet.

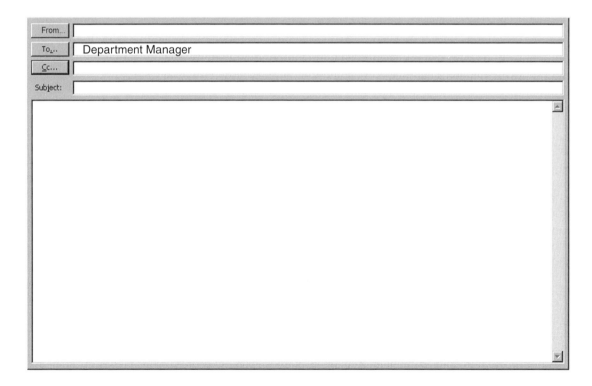

From...	
To...	Department Manager
Cc...	
Subject:	

PART TWO

Question 47

- Read the advertisement below written by Karen Petersen, who is looking for business premises.

Wanted: Business Premises

I am a local businesswoman who intends to open an internet café and I am looking for premises. If you have a building for rent which may be suitable, please contact me with details.

Karen Petersen

PO Box 53

- Write a **letter** to Ms Petersen:
  - informing her that you own a suitable building
  - describing the facilities the building has
  - explaining where the building is located
  - saying when the building is available.
- Write **60–80** words on your Answer Sheet.
- Do not include any postal addresses.

LISTENING   Approximately 40 minutes (including 10 minutes' transfer time)

LISTENING

PART ONE

Questions 1–8

- For questions **1–8** you will hear eight short recordings.
- For each question, mark **one** letter (**A**, **B** or **C**) for the correct answer.

Example:

Who is Emily going to write to?

A   the staff
B   the supplier
C   the clients

The answer is **A**.

- After you have listened once, replay each recording.

1   Which chart shows last week's production figures?

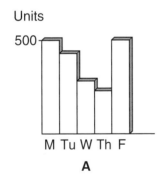

Units

A

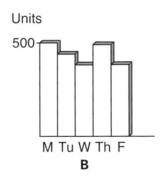

Units

B

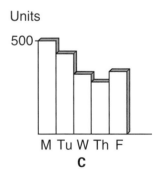

Units

C

2   Which floor is the Committee Room on?

first floor	second floor	third floor
A	**B**	**C**

3   How many Execujet flights are there to Ireland each day?

7

A

25

B

40

C

4   Which radio report is on first?

A   Big Interview
B   Business News
C   Money Savers

5   Which is the new packaging?

                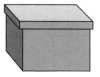

A   **B**   **C**

6   Which benefit will the client receive?

A   faster delivery
B   larger discounts
C   longer credit period

7 Which chart shows Freebird's market share for last year?

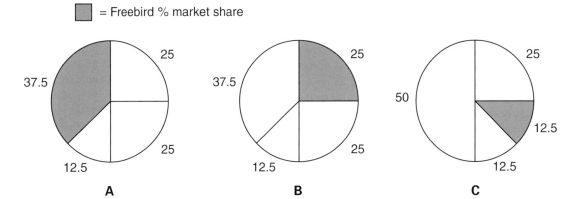

8 When will Mr Richards receive the new photocopier?

today	tomorrow	next week
A	**B**	**C**

PART TWO

Questions 9–15

- Look at the quotation below.
- Some information is missing.
- You will hear a sales manager giving a secretary information to include in the quotation.
- For each question (**9–15**), fill in the missing information in the numbered space using a **word**, **numbers** or **letters**.
- After you have listened once, replay the recording.

Cowdray Textiles

216–220 Handsworth Road
Sheffield, S9 3JP
Tel: 0114 272 7937

QUOTATION

QUOTATION REFERENCE:	(9) .... (Please state when telephoning)
TO:	(10) .... Ltd Campfield Retail Park Rotherham, S60 4BR
ITEM:	(11) .... rolls white patterned cotton
PRODUCT NAME:	(12) ....
PAYMENT TERMS:	(13) .... days
DISCOUNT:	(14) .... %
TOTAL AMOUNT:	(15) £ ....

PART THREE

Questions 16–22

- Look at the notes about changes in a company.
- Some information is missing.
- You will hear part of a talk by a manager to members of staff.
- For each question (**16–22**), fill in the missing information in the numbered space using **one** or **two** words.
- After you have listened once, replay the recording.

Company Changes

Company will merge with (16) .... International

Site to be sold: (17) ....

Move to new Head Office in (18) .... next year

New company name: (19) ....

Company logo will be (20) ....

Benefits for staff:

Opportunities to work in
branch located in (21) ....

Staff Development
Programme – first course: (22) .... training

PART FOUR

Questions 23–30

- You will hear a discussion between James Pierce and Susanna White, talking about their company's current advertising campaign for a new range of convenience foods.
- For each question (**23–30**), mark **one** letter (**A**, **B** or **C**) for the correct answer.
- After you have listened once, replay the recording.

23 Who appeared in the advertisements for the new products?

    A   agency actors
    B   company employees
    C   famous people

24 Consumers have described the advertisements as

    A   fashionable.
    B   amusing.
    C   unusual.

25 Since the campaign started, sales have been

    A   higher than predicted.
    B   exactly as predicted.
    C   lower than predicted.

26 Susanna says the largest consumer group for these products is

    A   teenagers.
    B   women.
    C   men.

27 According to the survey, most consumers have seen the ads in

    A   *Food Ideas.*
    B   *Healthy Eating.*
    C   *Easy Meals.*

28 What does James say about the advertising agency's charges?

    A   They are not good value for money.
    B   They plan to charge more for their services.
    C   It is worth paying their high charges.

29 The agency recommends continuing the current advertising campaign for

    A   one month more.
    B   two months more.
    C   three months more.

30 James suggests that the company should also advertise in

    A   national newspapers.
    B   sports magazines.
    C   cinema guides.

You now have 10 minutes to transfer your answers to your Answer Sheet.

SPEAKING   12 minutes

SAMPLE SPEAKING TASKS

PART ONE

The interview – about 2 minutes

In this part the interlocutor asks questions to each of the candidates in turn. You have to give information about yourself and express personal opinions.

PART TWO

'Mini presentation' – about 5 minutes

In this part of the test you are asked to give a short talk on a business topic. You have to choose one of the topics from the two below and then talk for about one minute. You have one minute to prepare your ideas.

A   WHAT IS IMPORTANT WHEN . . .?

ARRANGING A BUSINESS TRIP ABROAD

- TYPE OF TRANSPORT
- ACCOMMODATION
- CONTACT PERSON

B   WHAT IS IMPORTANT WHEN . . .?

CHOOSING OFFICES TO RENT

- LOCATION
- FACILITIES
- COST

PART THREE

Discussion – about 5 minutes

In this part of the test the examiner reads out a scenario and gives you some prompt material in the form of pictures or words. You have 30 seconds to look at the prompt card, an example of which is below, and then about two minutes to discuss the scenario with your partner. After that the examiner will ask you more questions related to the topic.

For **two** or **three** candidates

Scenario

> I'm going to describe a situation.
>
> **The Managing Director of a large international company needs to appoint a new Personal Assistant. Talk together for about two minutes about two of the people who have applied for the post and decide which one would be more suitable.**
>
> Here are some ideas to help you.

Prompt material

Ms Kazu Suzuki

Age:	30
Status:	Single
Nationality:	Japanese

Current post:	Personal Assistant
Experience:	10 years' office work
Qualifications:	IT Certificate
Personal qualities:	Good organisational & communication skills
Foreign languages:	English, Korean

Mr Robert Brown

Age:	22
Status:	Single
Nationality:	American

Current post:	Temporary secretary
Experience:	4 years' general office duties
Qualifications:	Diploma in Business Studies
Personal qualities:	Good team member, & keen to learn
Foreign language:	Spanish

Follow-on questions

- If you interviewed a candidate, what question would you ask? (Why?)

- What makes someone a good Personal Assistant? (Why?)

- Which do you think is more important when appointing staff, experience or willingness to learn? (Why?)

- Is it better to have more than one interviewer at job interviews? (Why/Why not?)

- What questions should applicants ask at interview? (Why?)

KEY

Test 1 Reading

Part 1

1 C   2 A   3 B   4 C   5 B

Part 2

6 D   7 B   8 H   9 E   10 G

Part 3

11 G   12 F   13 B   14 D   15 A

Part 4

16 A   17 C   18 B   19 B   20 C
21 B   22 A

Part 5

23 B   24 A   25 B   26 A   27 C
28 B

Part 6

29 C   30 A   31 B   32 C   33 A
34 C   35 B   36 A   37 B   38 A
39 C   40 B

Part 7

41 CUSTOMER SERVICES
42 ROGER WHITE   43 (AN) OVAL TABLE
44 (A) (LARGE) SCREEN   45 PARKING
    (FOR 9 (PEOPLE/CARS)) / (9) (CAR)
    PARKING SPACES

Test 1 Writing

Part 1

Sample A

> To   Line Manager
> C.c   Carole
> Subject   Sales Report
>
> I'm sorry for the delay about the latest sales figure.
>
> I had to prepare our next meeting asking all the staff if they'll come, booking hotel and so on.
>
> The report will be ready within two next weeks.
> Yours sincerly,

Band 5
Very good attempt – clear and with minimal errors.

Sample B

> My report for my latest sales figures is not yet ready! I need a delay to done it perfectly. I thing that I can do it for Monday (in four days).
>
> Thanks,

Band 2
This answer is limited to a Band 2 as it fails to achieve the first and second content points.

Part 2

Sample C

> Dear Ms Lambert,
>
> Thank you for your letter about details of Business Management course.
>
> There would be 75 person on the course. Unfortunately, we will not be able to inform you the date yet, as we are planning to organise an exhibition in summer season. As soon as we arrange the date of exhibition, we will inform you when we are going to start.
>
> We wondered whether any chance to have a discount when we attend the course over then 50 person. Could you please send us some information about discounts?
>
> We look forward to hearing from you soon.
>
> Yours sincerely,

Band 5
This answer represents a full realisation of the task; the content is confidently organised and expressed with only a few non-impeding errors.

Sample D

> Dear Ms Lambert
>
> I thank you for your letter.
>
> It's possibly there are nine sportsmen and six sportswomen on the course.
>
> I apologise me but I don't know actually the date of the course. It's probably that the course begins in few months but I don't know precisely.
>
> I keep you at your concience the last year bill for seventeen persons, and I hope that the price won't be change.
>
> Yours faithfully

Band 2
In addition to idiosyncratic phrasing and a number of errors, this answer fails to achieve the third and fourth content points so can only score a maximum Band 2.

Test 1   Listening

Part 1

1 A   2 C   3 A   4 B   5 A   6 C
7 B   8 B

Part 2

9 BAKER
10 RKS
11 54453
12 14(TH)
13 12(%)
14 987413
15 CULLERS

Part 3

16 WINTER
17 RADIOS
18 OFFICE
19 NEW YORK
20 (OUR) (VERY OWN) CREDIT CARD(S)
21 COMMERCIAL
22 ACCOUNT MANAGEMENT

Part 4

23 B   24 C   25 B   26 C   27 A
28 B   29 A   30 C

Tapescript

Listening Test 1

This is the Business English Certificate Preliminary 2, Listening Test 1.

[pause]

Part One. Questions 1 to 8.

For questions 1–8 you will hear eight short recordings. For each question, mark one letter (A, B or C) for the correct answer.

Here is an example: When were the machine parts sent?

[pause]

Woman: Mr Hooper rang. He needs those parts for the packing machine by the third.
Man: Well, it's already the first today . . . but wait . . . no, it's OK. They were sent out on the thirty-first.
Woman: Good. He'll certainly get them by the third, then.

[pause]

The answer is A.

Now we are ready to start.

After you have listened once, replay each recording.

[pause]

One: Why does the woman want the job?

[pause]

Woman: I'm applying for that job in the Marketing Department, I'm tired of going all the way to Head Office every day! The Marketing office is just down the road from my house.
Man: Mmm, you'd save money on train fares . . . But it's only the same salary!
Woman: I know, but I want to use my computer skills as well.

[pause]

Two: When is the trade fair?

[pause]

Next year's trade fair in Milan, usually the first week of June, is now on June the twenty-sixth and twenty-seventh. Its organisers are not happy – they were hoping that the fair would be on the twelfth and thirteenth. However, the situation in . . .

[pause]

Three: What is the purpose of today's meeting?

[pause]

Woman: When are you seeing Munro International about signing the distribution contract?
Man: Well, I'm meeting two of their directors today for lunch so I'll make a date to do that then.
Woman: Fine. Are you going to talk about the merger over lunch?
Man: That's the aim. When I asked our MD for his advice on the next step, he suggested this lunch meeting.

[pause]

Four: Which chart shows this year's sales?

[pause]

Man: Looking at our main markets, Asia now represents fifty per cent of all sales. Europe and the USA are the other two main players, with sales in the USA at thirty-eight per cent, unlike last year when Europe had the bigger share.

[pause]

Five: How much will Emma's hotel bill be?

[pause]

Woman(1): Hello, it's Emma MacDonald here from AB Electronics. I'd like to book a single room for the twenty-fifth please.
Woman(2): Certainly. Single rooms are seventy-two pounds fifty per night, including breakfast.
Woman(1): Oh . . . I see but my company uses the hotel regularly. We normally get a discount.
Woman(2): Oh sorry. That'll be sixty pounds per night then, sixty-five pounds fifty with breakfast.
Woman(1): Oh, I won't want breakfast.

[pause]

Six: What will the finance company give advice about?

[pause]

. . . Call Walker's Finance Company now. We are specialists in advising successful small businesses on aspects of business finance. So, if you want to attract investment or reduce your company's tax bill, call us on 0207 765 5540 . . .

[pause]

Seven: Which graph are they looking at?

[pause]

Man: Look at this graph. There's a real problem with production at this plant. Over the last two years we've increased our investment in it considerably – here, see?
Woman: Mm, that's true.
Man: And yet production continues at the same level . . .
Woman: You're right. There's been no fall in production, but there should be a rise – and there isn't.

[pause]

Eight: What's the problem with the seminar?

[pause]

Woman: Dan.
Man: Yes.
Woman: Um, slight problem with the time management seminar next week.
Man: Don't tell me – Andy Norton can't give the introductory talk . . . and I've got to do it.
Woman: It's not that. There's such a huge demand this time. I've had over sixty bookings and the venue is only big enough for forty. It's funny, last time we had so few bookings.

[pause]

That is the end of Part One.

[pause]

Part Two. Questions 9 to 15.

Look at the notes below.

Some information is missing.

You will hear a man telephoning a sports centre.

For each question 9–15, fill in the missing information in the numbered space using a word, numbers or letters.

After you have listened once, replay the recording.

You now have ten seconds to look at the notes.

[pause]

Now listen, and fill in the missing information.

Woman: Ace Sports Centre. Can I help you?

Man: I hope so. We're supposed to be customers of yours, but I've just seen your opening date's delayed again.

Woman: Oh, er . . . could I take your name please?

Man: Yes, Charles Baker.

Woman: And are you an individual member, sir?

Man: No – I'm the Human Resources manager at RKS Limited.

Woman: That's the letters R–K–S?

Man: Yes, that's right. We've got twenty members registered with you.

Woman: Were you given a membership number?

Man: Yes, it's 5-double-4-5-3. But I need to know when we can start using the facilities.

Woman: Yes. We're so sorry about the delay. But we are arranging special tours for corporate members in November, to introduce you to the facilities . . .

Man: When would that be?

Woman: Thursdays . . . Could some of you make the next one, on the seventh?

Man: That'd be difficult but the thirteenth'd be . . .

Woman: Er, the fourteenth . . .

Man: OK . . .

Woman: Starting at six?

Man: Sure. I'll see who'd be free that evening.

Woman: Because of the delay, we'd like to suggest a fee reduction . . .

Man: Yes, we'd expect at least ten per cent . . .

Woman: Actually, we'd thought twelve . . .

Man: That seems very reasonable . . . thanks.

Woman: Great. Can I just confirm your phone number . . . 01332 987987?

Man: Use my direct line, 987413.

Woman: Or email?

Man: Yes . . . better . . . info-at-cullers-dot-com.

Woman: At?

Man: C-U-double-L-E-R-S dot com.

Woman: I'll be in touch tomorrow . . .

[pause]

Now listen to the recording again.

[pause]

That is the end of Part Two. You now have ten seconds to check your answers.

[pause]

Part Three. Questions 16 to 22.

Look at the notes below.

Some information is missing.

You will hear part of a report by the company's chairman.

For each question 16–22, fill in the missing information in the numbered space using one or two words.

After you have listened once, replay the recording.

You have ten seconds to look at the notes.

[pause]

Now listen, and complete the notes.

Man: . . . and the other announcement about company personnel concerns Managing Director, Bob Jones. Bob retires next month after twelve years of service. He will, however, continue to act as part-time consultant. His replacement as MD is another Bob . . . Bob Winter, currently Head of Operations.

Now, I'd like to summarise our performance last year, before moving on to plans for 2003. I've decided that every year we should introduce a competition to guess the best-selling product throughout our stores. It's never been the same for two years running. For example, in 2000 it was mobile phones. The following year record sales of radios were achieved. I'm quite surprised, especially as we'd predicted it would be electronic organisers. (Any feedback on this idea would be welcome.)

Recent investment in our furniture department has resulted in great improvements in sales: this includes children's, garden and, most dramatically, office furniture, which doubled its sales volume last year.

Now to the announcement of the most successful branch. Our Paris branch has held this position for two years, but now it's the turn of New York, with the London branch in second place.

Looking to the future, we're planning a number of developments. Our Personal Loan Service received much praise from customers when it was brought in last year. In response to customer demand, we're now going to launch our own credit card next year, as well as other financial services in years to come.

Moving on to new stores. As you will

remember, twelve months ago, we closed some of our unprofitable High Street stores. I still think we took the right decision – and next year, we've decided to locate six branches in commercial centres. That's the same number we've already opened in new shopping centres – it'll be interesting to compare their performance.

Finally, as part of our continuous programme of staff development, we plan to offer a wider variety of courses next year, including Account Management, as well as continuing with IT Skills and Customer Services.

Now . . .

[pause]

Now listen to the recording again.

[pause]

That is the end of Part Three. You now have 20 seconds to check your answers.

[pause]

Part Four. Questions 23 to 30.

You will hear a discussion between two managers, Matthew and Angela, about some problems with staff.

For each question 23–30, mark one letter (A, B or C) for the correct answer.

After you have listened once, replay the recording.

You have 45 seconds to read through the questions.

[pause]

Now listen, and mark A, B or C.

Man: Hello Angela. What's wrong? You don't look very cheerful!

Woman: Hi Matthew. No, I'm not very pleased. I've just heard Phil Jones, one of my junior managers, has handed in his resignation!

Man: Hmm. One of the managers in my department resigned three days ago – and then there were two who left in June.

Woman: What's wrong with them? Don't they like working here?

Man: Oh, it's not that. We always have dozens of applicants for junior management posts.

Woman: Yes, because they know they can get good experience here that'll be useful in the future.

Man: Right. And once they've gained some experience with us, they can get a better-paid job somewhere else.

Woman: You're right, I know, but why is it always about the money?

Man: Lots of people are like that now. I suppose these junior managers are no different . . . But you know . . . I think they shouldn't be in such a hurry to leave. They know the company likes to keep staff who are good at their jobs, and there are plenty of opportunities for promotion if they stay longer than two years.

Woman: Mmm. You know the most annoying thing?

Man: All the hours we spend going through CVs and interviewing for new staff . . . ?

Woman: That's part of it. I admit I do get bored doing interviews when you know the person's not right for the job. No, what really annoys me most is the time I spend showing new employees how to do the job. Really, it takes hours, weeks.

Man: Maybe we need a review of our recruitment policy. Maybe we are taking on the wrong sort of people. At that conference I went to last month, they said that it's often harder work for a junior manager to join a team of employees if the team got on well with the old manager. The team may decide they don't like the way of working and they may decide to resign too.

Woman: Yeah, people sometimes forget how many problems it can cause by even employing one person who is wrong for the company. I don't just mean the cost of recruiting a replacement.

Man: Maybe Personnel would let us use an employment agency in future.

Woman: I don't think they would, but I have heard they might give applicants who come for interview some sort of personality test.

Man: Really! You know some companies employ people who analyse the handwriting of anyone applying for a job.

Woman: It's funny you mention that. I was reading an article yesterday about how companies in America do that . . . to find out how smart applicants are, how motivated they are to succeed, how much self-confidence they have, and so on.

Man: How can the way you write prove how clever you are? What nonsense! Perhaps what we need to do here is look more carefully at the CVs we receive – maybe we're not even interviewing the right kind of person. It could even be that our job ads don't attract the right people.

Woman: I'm not sure about that. We're basically happy with our junior managers. It's just that some of them don't seem to stay as long as we'd like.

Man: Well, maybe we do need a different procedure when we meet the applicants at interview.

Woman: Yes, I think you're right about that. Let's fix up a meeting with Personnel to . . .

[pause]

Now listen to the recording again.

[pause]

That is the end of Part Four. You now have ten minutes to transfer your answers to your Answer Sheet.

Note: Teacher, stop the recording here and time ten minutes. Remind students when there is **one** minute remaining.

[pause]

That is the end of the test.

Test 2   Reading

Part 1

1 C   2 A   3 B   4 B   5 A

Part 2

6 G   7 E   8 B   9 A   10 C

Part 3

11 D   12 C   13 H   14 G   15 E

Part 4

16 B   17 C   18 B   19 A   20 C
21 B   22 A

Part 5

23 A   24 C   25 A   26 B   27 C
28 B

Part 6

29 B   30 A   31 C   32 C   33 C
34 B   35 C   36 A   37 A   38 A
39 B   40 A

Part 7

41 LAURA GRAVES
42 STAFF DEVELOPMENT
(DEPT/DEPARTMENT)
43 655   44 KAREN HILL/K. HILL
45 INTERNET STRATEGIES (COURSE)

Test 2   Writing

Part 1

Sample A

> We've duly received the telephone complaint by Mr. White about the late deliveries caused by shipping problems.
>
> In order to expedite the procedures, it shall be better to arrange someone to discuss with the customs straight away.

Band 4
All content points have been dealt with in this script but the phrasing requires some effort on the part of the reader, preventing it receiving a Band 5.

Sample B

> To Mr. Miller, Customer Service Manager
>
> I made a complaint about late deliveries. We have a problem about our supplier. The supplier had a fire in the stock and the goods are bad. We will receive the goods next week and we will write a letter to our customer that he will get your goods next week. Best regards

Band 2
The scenario has not been fully understood in this answer and as a result only one content point has been dealt with, limiting this to a Band 2.

Part 2

Sample C

```
23. Nov. 2002

Dear Ms Reeves

Thank you for your letter regarding the
presentation at your meeting on 15ᵗʰ December.

I'm very sorry, but I'm unable to attend this
meeting. In Stuttgart there is a fair I have to be
present from 13ᵗʰ December to 17ᵗʰ December.

I would suggest an appointment in January. The
15ᵗʰ January is a day I will be available all time.

If you agree please contact my secretary Gina
Johnes by 0172/55555 to confirm the date.

We looking forward to hearing from you soon.

Your sincerely
```

Band 5

Although not entirely free of errors, none of these
is impeding and the response is clear and well
organised, covering all the content points.

Sample D

```
Dear Ms Reeves

Sorry, but I can not attend the meeting, because
I am on 15ᵗʰ December on holiday. Of course I
would give a short presentation about new
advertising in your department. I could hold the
presentation on 15ᵗʰ January next year. Please
give me the contact from your secretary to
confirm the arrangements.

Yours faithfully
```

Band 3

The range of language used in this response is
adequate, as is its cohesion and organisation;
however the final content point has not been
achieved.

Test 2   Listening

Part 1

1 A	2 B	3 A	4 C	5 B
6 C	7 B	8 A		

Part 2

9 28 (SQ M)
10 (£)645
11 7500
12 GRESHAM
13 250
14 10.30
15 TF62880

Part 3

16 CARTWRIGHT
17 TOP FLOOR
18 ACCOUNTS (OFFICE)
19 MARKETING
20 THURSDAY
21 (PLASTIC) CARD
22 (AN) APPLICATION FORM

Part 4

23 A	24 B	25 B	26 C	27 A
28 A	29 C	30 B		

Tapescript

Listening Test Two

*This is the Business English Certificate Preliminary
2, Listening Test 2.*

[pause]

Part One. Questions 1 to 8.

*For questions 1–8, you will hear eight short
recordings. For each question, mark one letter (A,
B or C) for the correct answer.*

*Here's an example: When were the machine parts
sent?*

[pause]

Woman: Mr Hooper rang. He needs those parts
for the packing machine by the third.
Man: Well, it's already the first today . . . but wait
. . . no, it's OK. They were sent out on the
thirty-first.
Woman: Good. He'll certainly get them by the
third, then.

[pause]

The answer is A.

Now we are ready to start.

After you have listened once, replay each recording.

[pause]

One: Why is the man late for the meeting?

[pause]

Woman: Sorry we had to start the meeting without you. What happened – train late again?

Man: It was, but only by a few minutes. According to my diary, we're not starting till eleven.

Woman: We were, but I've got to fly out to the Tokyo office on urgent business this afternoon, so we had to bring the meeting forward.

Man: Well, no-one told me . . .

[pause]

Two: Why is Timtex performing badly?

[pause]

Woman: Timtex isn't doing too well, is it? I see profits are right down again.

Man: Mm. Well, at the moment the market's sharply divided between those who want fashionable clothing, even though it costs a lot, and those who want to pay as little as possible. So by aiming at the middle market, Timtex doesn't really please anyone very much.

[pause]

Three: Which graph shows the company's sales?

[pause]

Man: . . . and despite a slight fall early in the year, WP Engineering have in fact done well this year, with a steady rise in sales up to now, which their Managing Director, William Peters, hopes will continue into next year . . .

[pause]

Four: Where do they decide to hold the seminar?

[pause]

Woman: Where are we holding the seminar this year?

Man: How about that new hotel in town?

Woman: It's too expensive for our budget . . . somewhere like the conference centre is more suitable – it's fully booked though.

Man: And everyone complained about the Trade Club last year . . .

Woman: OK, well maybe we should spend more on the venue this year. Let's go with your idea.

[pause]

Five: What does the successful business produce?

[pause]

Woman: These articles about new businesses are interesting.

Man: Especially the one about the woman whose company sells a game she invented herself.

Woman: Mm. She's doing really well. The one that made soft drinks failed within six months.

Man: Yes. And the people publishing the magazine did well at first, but then they couldn't find any more investors.

Woman: Pity. Seemed a good idea.

[pause]

Six: In which department does Ben work now?

[pause]

Woman: Hello Karl! How are you?

Man: I'm fine thanks. How are things at the company?

Woman: Oh, there have been so many changes since you left!

Man: I hear Ben's moved?

Woman: Yes . . . they needed someone with an engineering qualification in Marketing, so they transferred him there.

Man: Who's replaced him in Sales then?

Woman: No-one yet!

[pause]

Seven: Which chart shows the bank's current network of branches?

[pause]

Man: . . . at the moment a quarter of the bank's branches are in Europe, and a third in Asia. The rest of their business is, of course, in the States. But today's news is that they're planning to close some US branches . . .

[pause]

Eight: What do they still need to put in the hall?

[pause]

Man: I've just been over to the hall to check the arrangements for the shareholders' meeting

Woman: Is everything set up OK?

Man: Almost. They haven't got the microphone in yet. Everything else was all right though . . . the OHP was there . . .

Woman: What about the video player?

Man: Oh, we changed our minds about that, so I didn't book one in the end.

[pause]

That is the end of Part One.

[pause]

Part Two. Questions 9 to 15.

Look at the form below.

Some information is missing.

You will hear a woman booking exhibition space on the phone.

For each question 9–15, fill in the missing information in the numbered space using a word, numbers or letters.

After you have listened once, replay the recording.

You have ten seconds to look at the form.

[pause]

Now listen, and write the missing information.

Woman: Hello, yes, I'm phoning from Altrex. Could I book a space for next June's trade fair?
Man: Certainly. The units are ten, twenty-eight or forty square metres.
Woman: Well, our stand is fifteen square metres . . .
Man: So you need twenty-eight. There're plenty that size in Hall D – or one left in A.
Woman: How much would that one be?
Man: Six hundred and forty five pounds. Units in D are four hundred and eighty.
Woman: Make it the one in Hall A – the more expensive one! How many people are you expecting? I heard this year was a bit disappointing?
Man: Yes, it was – but we did have six thousand. Next year we're planning for seven and a half thousand.
Woman: Good. Now, we also need a conference room.
Man: Fine, I could offer you the Gresham Room . . .
Woman: Can you spell the name?
Man: G-R-E-S-H-A-M. There's also the Ferris Room, that's larger. It holds four hundred.
Woman: How many seats are there in the Gresham Room?
Man: It takes two hundred and fifty.
Woman: That's plenty. Can we have the room from ten or ten-thirty?

Man: Let's make it half past. Would a twelve o'clock finish be OK?
Woman: Perfect.
Man: Now, the room reference number is IMO5734 and the whole booking is on TF62880. Use that if you contact us.

[pause]

Now listen to the recording again.

[pause]

That is the end of Part Two. You now have ten seconds to check your answers.

[pause]

Part Three. Questions 16 to 22.

Look at the notes below.

Some information is missing.

You will hear part of a talk given to a group of new employees.

For each question 16–22, fill in the missing information in the numbered space using one or two words.

After you have listened once, replay the recording.

You have ten seconds to look at the notes.

[pause]

Now listen, and complete the form.

Woman: Welcome to NYP. You know already how valuable your skills will be to us as we expand – I believe you have fifteen different languages between you.

There are three of us in Personnel and I'm the one you should come to for any help or information. The other two are Ben Gillick and Max Collins, and my name is Sarah Cartwright that's C-A-R-T-W-R-I-G-H-T. I'd just like to give you a few practical details now, before the MD comes to talk to you.

Firstly, the canteen on the ground floor is open all day for coffee, meals, etc, but there are also coffee machines on the top floor, where we have all the company noticeboards, so staff often meet there to talk.

Um, next, some of you have asked about your tax position . . . and for any tax questions, you need to contact the Accounts Office. General salary enquiries can be made to the Finance Office itself.

Two events, now. Today, in the conference

room, at three-thirty, there'll be a presentation –
it's not on new developments as the notices say,
it's actually on marketing. You're welcome to
attend to see how we're moving in that area.
There'll also be a buffet lunch for all staff
working on the new projects – that includes you,
that's on Wednesday – sorry, I mean Thursday –
you'll get full details later.

Finally, sometimes you'll need to use the
machines in the print room. The first time you
go in there, register for a plastic card – you don't
need it for ordinary photocopiers, but you do
for the colour ones.

The other thing to sign up for, if you want to,
is the sports club, just two minutes from here. If
you're interested, see Max Collins, who'll give
you an application form.

Right, that's all for the moment. Here's coffee,
and the MD is just coming through now.

[pause]

Now listen to the recording again.

[pause]

*That is the end of Part Three. You now have 20
seconds to check your answers.*

[pause]

Part Four. Questions 23 to 30.

*You will hear a conversation between two senior
managers of a large company based in the UK.
They are talking about a visit to the company by a
group of foreign executives.*

*For each question 23–30, mark one letter (A, B or
C) for the correct answer.*

After you have listened once, replay the recording.

You have 45 seconds to read through the questions.

[pause]

Now listen, and mark A, B or C.

Man: Come in, Diana. Coffee?
Woman: Thank you, Michael.
Man: Now, about this visit by the senior
executives from Poland . . .
Woman: Mm. Do we know when they're coming?
Man: We offered them three choices – the end of
March, the middle of April and the beginning of
May.
Woman: Yes . . .
Man: And they chose the earliest one, which is
good, actually, with the review coming up in May.

Woman: True. But we do need definite dates. And
how many are coming? There were six of them
last time. Did you say about eight? My P.A.
needs to make firm bookings for their
accommodation now – otherwise it'll be very
difficult to find a hotel.
Man: You're right. They said six to eight
originally, but I've had an email this morning
saying it's going to be seven. Now we've got a
definite number, we can make all the other
bookings for them.
Woman: Good, that gives us eight weeks until
they come.
Man: Right, well, here are my suggestions for their
schedule. Mm . . . They'll be with the company
for four days. On the first day I think they
should visit one of our main sites. So, it should
be either the company headquarters, or the retail
outlets in the area, or the factory in Swindon.
Woman: I definitely think we should bring them
here to the headquarters on the second day. I
don't think they need to see the shops at all.
Man: OK, we'll show them the production line
then – hopefully they'll be impressed.
Woman: Right, I'll arrange that.
Man: What we've got to remember, of course, is
that this group have a particular interest in
coming here.
Woman: Mm . . . Isn't it to look at our new
computer systems?
Man: Well, in fact, on this trip they want to look
at workplace procedures, you know – health
and safety, employer–employee relations, things
like that. Not our performance figures – though
they'll see those when they come here to
headquarters, of course.
Woman: And who will they meet while they're
here?
Man: Well, the Managing Director. And you and
me, obviously . . .
Woman: And have they said who they're interested
in seeing? The Customer Relations staff, maybe?
Man: Perhaps, but definitely the people
responsible for developing the company's
Human Resources strategy.
Woman: Right, we'll get the manager and his
team to organise something then.
Man: Mm . . . Now – the presentation.
Woman: Yes. The afternoon of the second day.
The basic organisation for that is already in
place, in fact.
Man: Good!
Woman: Simon's going to do the presentation.
Man: What's he going to talk about?

Woman: Something on our various schemes for rewarding staff – the new profit-sharing scheme, bonuses and so on.

Man: Right. That'll fit in nicely. Simon's very competent, of course – there's plenty of time to negotiate all that in detail. Now, for the third day, they've made their own arrangements in London. They're going to see some key Members of Parliament – they want to talk about trade agreements.

Woman: That sounds interesting . . .

Man: They wanted to see one of the new commercial developments in the city but there wasn't time to arrange that.

Woman: Oh, I see. There isn't an official government reception for the group, is there?

Man: Not this time.

Woman: OK . . . What about their last day? I understand they've asked to go somewhere different.

Man: Yes. I'd like to take them to Scotland. There're a lot of developments there we could show them.

Woman: Oh, isn't that too far for one day?

Man: Unfortunately, it is. But they could fly up to the North East to the factory there.

Woman: Why not the exhibition centre in Birmingham? That's much closer!

Man: They went there last time, remember?

Woman: Of course. I'm sure they'll like your idea. If you like, I could find out about flights to the regional airport there.

Man: Yes, thanks. Now, can we just . . .

[pause]

Now listen to the recording again.

[pause]

That is the end of Part Four. You now have ten minutes to transfer your answers to your Answer Sheet.

Note: Teacher, stop the recording here and time ten minutes. Remind students when there is **one** minute remaining.

[pause]

That is the end of the test.

Test 3   Reading

Part 1

| 1 B | 2 A | 3 C | 4 A | 5 C |

Part 2

| 6 H | 7 C | 8 G | 9 A | 10 E |

Part 3

| 11 F | 12 H | 13 D | 14 C | 15 A |

Part 4

| 16 A | 17 B | 18 A | 19 C | 20 B |
| 21 C | 22 A | | | |

Part 5

| 23 C | 24 B | 25 B | 26 A | 27 B |
| 28 C | | | | |

Part 6

29 A	30 C	31 C	32 B	33 A
34 B	35 A	36 C	37 C	38 A
39 B	40 C			

Part 7

41 ALAN BLACKMAN   42 3/THREE
43 MONTHLY / EVERY MONTH / ONCE A MONTH   44 (BY) EMAIL
45 COMPUTER TODAY (MAGAZINE)

Test 3   Writing

Part 1

Sample A

> I agree to write this article. I would like you know that I will write about the company's economic situation and its future. I would like to know what deadline it has. I look forward your answer.
>
> Thanks.

Band 5
Although this response contains one or two errors these do not cause the reader undue effort and all the content points are achieved.

Sample B

> to: Bill Evans, Personnel Manager
>
> I'm agree to write the article for the company magazine. I'm thinking to ask about they experience on website and for additional service. I would like to know when the deadline is for the article.

Band 3
This response does not adequately deal with the second content point – giving brief details of the article – limiting it to a Band 3.

Part 2

Sample C

> Dear Mr Hutton,
>
> I am very grateful for your recent letter. the reason of this delay is due to the last delivery of our products.
>
> First of all, I am very unhappy because the last products that you sent us was damaged and we could use them.
>
> Secondly, I will make you a new order if you promise me that the new products do not be damaged. However, I would like you send me an up-to-date catalogue of products.
>
> Finally, I want to say you that I want a 20% of discount in the products.
>
> If you have any doubts do not hesitate to contact me.
>
> Yours sincerely,

Band 4
Although all the content points have been achieved in this response, there are numerous errors and despite the fact that most of these are non-impeding the effect on the reader is not entirely positive.

Sample D

> Dear Mr Hutton.
>
> Thank you for you letter. We havent placed an order because the quality of your last delivery products were not success for what we need as usual and some of the products have damaged when it arrived.
>
> Can you send me an up-to-date catalogue from your company? I would like to have 10% discount on my next order.
>
> Please contact us if you got any problem.
>
> Yours sincerely,

Band 3
Although this response achieves all four content points, there are a number of errors and the range of language and structure are only adequate, especially in the first half of the response.

Test 3   Listening

Part 1

1 A	2 C	3 B	4 A	5 B	6 C
7 B	8 B				

Part 2

9 JY836X
10 95 (CM)
11 104 (CM)
12 14
13 680
14 7
15 DOUGHTY

Part 3

16 ELECTRICAL GOODS
17 OXFORD
18 AUSTRIA
19 JANUARY
20 (A/THE) (COMPANY) PENSION
21 MANAGEMENT TRAINING
22 (UNIVERSITY) GRADUATES

Part 4

23 A	24 B	25 A	26 B	27 C
28 B	29 B	30 C		

Tapescript

Listening Test 3

This is the Business English Certificate Preliminary 2, Listening Test 3.

[pause]

Part One. Questions 1 to 8.

For questions 1–8, you will hear eight short recordings. For each question, mark one letter (A, B or C) for the correct answer.

Here is an example: Who is Emily going to write to?

[pause]

Man: Emily, that supplier we use has become very unreliable, and we've decided to look for another one.
Woman: Seems a good idea.
Man: We don't need to inform our clients, but could you send a note round to all our departments when we've decided who to replace the supplier with?
Woman: Yes, of course.

[pause]

The answer is A.

Now we are ready to start.

After you have listened once, replay each recording.

[pause]

One: Who does the man need to speak to?

[pause]

Man: Hello. John Vernon here. I had a meeting last Friday with one of your production engineers, Peter Tribe. He said the person who'd really be able to help me would be Charles Pearson. Could you ask him to ring me?

[pause]

Two: Where is the man telephoning from?

[pause]

Man: Oh, Amy, I'm glad you haven't left the office yet! I need the sales budget report urgently for tomorrow's meeting.
Woman: OK . . . where shall I send it?
Man: Can you email it to me here at home? My email address is on my desk. It's next to the number of the hotel – you may need to contact me there tomorrow.

[pause]

Three: How many job applications have they received in total?

[pause]

Man: How was the jobs fair?
Woman: Ah, it was really successful! Over five hundred people an hour visited the show. I hope to be able to interview about a hundred of the three hundred people who've written in about the posts, though it will take at least two weeks to sort out all the applications.

[pause]

Four: How will the company carry out their market research?

[pause]

Woman: What's happening with the market research survey?
Man: Oh, there was some discussion about the best method to use.
Woman: Don't we always do telephone surveys?
Man: Yes, though I prefer talking to people face to face, but the MD says that's too expensive.
Woman: You could post the surveys.
Man: Well actually, we decided not to make any changes in the end.

[pause]

Five: Which graph is correct?

[pause]

Man: Over the past twelve months, shares in the new technology companies have risen, but not by as much as investors hoped. Their performance is disappointing as we'd expected them to do much better.

[pause]

Six: When is the woman going to take her holiday?

[pause]

Woman: We must sort out our holidays! I'd really like the first half of September . . .
Man: Er, I was thinking of going away during that time. We can't both be away at the same time.
Woman: I suppose I could go in July, or August, but . . .
Man: Don't worry! I'll go in August. You take the weeks you wanted – that's fine.

[pause]

Seven: What was the man's opinion of the presentation?

[pause]

Woman: Hi, Mike. What did you think of the presentation? I thought it was really excellent.
Man: I just couldn't get interested in it and I didn't really pay attention to what the speaker was saying.
Woman: Really? It was so clear, apart from anything else. All those figures can be really confusing.

[pause]

Eight: Which chart shows the company's turnover?

[pause]

Man: Turnover improved in 2002, didn't it?
Woman: Yes – though it was only slightly higher than 2001. The launch of Arial's new car really affected us. If their sales go on growing like that, it's going to be serious. Look at our drop in sales since 2000!
Man: So what are we going to do about it?

[pause]

That is the end of Part One.

[pause]

Part Two. Questions 9 to 15.

Look at the form below.

Some information is missing.

You will hear a man discussing an order for some factory equipment.

For each question 9–15, fill in the missing information in the numbered space using a word, numbers or letters.

After you have listened once, replay the recording.

You have ten seconds to look at the form.

[pause]

Now listen, and write the missing words, numbers or letters in the spaces.

Woman: L-R-S. Can I help you?
Man: Hello, I'm calling from Amstel Machine Tools. My colleague called last week about some factory workshop tables. The order reference number is . . . oh, sorry, just a second . . . I'll find it in a minute . . . ah, J-Y-8-3-6-X.

Woman: Ah . . . you didn't want the standard size, did you? Your colleague ordered ninety centimetres wide by two hundred and twelve centimetres long, didn't he?
Man: Well, I'm afraid we've had to change the layout of the workshop slightly, so, in fact, we need ninety-five by two hundred and twelve.
Woman: That's no problem.
Man: And we also want the tables to be six centimetres lower now . . . um, one hundred and four centimetres.
Woman: Is that for all fifteen tables? Sorry, you ordered fourteen, didn't you?
Man: We did. Can I just check the price with you?
Woman: Fine. It'll be six hundred and eighty pounds per table. The five hundred and twenty in the brochure is for the standard size.
Man: And we will still get five per cent discount on orders from you, won't we?
Woman: Actually, it went up to seven per cent in July. And is Mr Brown the contact name for the order?
Man: I think you need to change it to my name. That's Paul Doughty. Spelled D-O-U-G-H-T-Y.
Woman: OK. I'll give you a call as soon as the order's ready.
Man: Mm, thanks.

[pause]

Now listen to the recording again.

[pause]

That is the end of Part Two. You now have ten seconds to check your answers.

[pause]

Part Three. Questions 16 to 22.

Look at the notes below about a chain of department stores.

Some of the information is missing.

You will hear part of a talk given by the company's Human Resources manager.

For each question 16–22, fill in the missing information in the numbered spaces using one or two words or a number.

After you have listened once, replay the recording.

You have ten seconds to look at the notes.

[pause]

Now listen, and write the missing information in the spaces.

Man: Good morning. Thank you for your interest in working at Dennings Retail Group. Let me begin by telling you a little about Dennings. Then I'll talk about career opportunities with us.

As you know, Dennings is one of the leading chains of department stores in the country, best known for its electrical goods, which are responsible for roughly sixty per cent of our turnover. What you may not know is that the company began life as a furniture store, established in Birmingham in 1825.

There are now twenty-five stores in cities across Britain. The one we opened most recently is in Oxford, although the one everyone knows about – because of its amazing modern building – is in London. They all carry a wide range of goods.

The Dennings name is also expanding abroad. At the moment there are four stores outside the UK. The next one to open – in Austria – will join those already trading in Italy, Brazil, Malaysia and Canada.

Hopefully, customers in these and other countries will also begin to use Dennings Internet Shopping, when it's launched in January next year by the group. We're expecting these sales to equal the turnover of one of our smaller stores by December 2004.

This means we will need new staff in all areas of the company – and feel sure that the competitive salaries and the pension scheme we offer – open to all employees – will attract the best candidates.

We always encourage people inside the company to apply for internal promotion. In addition, we are looking for people for our management training course. This is for young people interested in a career with the company. We are also running a special introduction week called 'Getting to know Dennings' next month. This is something we do every year for university graduates who would like to find out about career opportunities at Dennings.

[pause]

Now listen to the recording again.

[pause]

That is the end of Part Three. You now have 20 seconds to check your answers.

[pause]

Part Four. Questions 23 to 30.

You will hear a radio interview. The interviewer is talking to a young businessman called James Osmond, who publishes a successful magazine called Day by Day.

For each question 23–30, mark one letter (A, B or C) for the correct answer.

After you have listened once, replay the recording.

You have 45 seconds to read through the questions.

[pause]

Now listen, and mark A, B or C.

Woman: 'I publish my own magazine, and it's very successful'. How many people, at just twenty-nine, can say that? Well, we have here a young businessman who can – he is James Osmond, the man behind the magazine *Day by Day*. Welcome, James.

Man: Hello.

Woman: James, did you think this magazine would be so successful, so quickly? I mean, two years ago, it was just an idea. Eighteen months ago, you still hadn't found anyone to provide the finance, but this week you're celebrating its first anniversary.

Man: No-one is more surprised than me.

Woman: Two years ago, you weren't even working in the media, were you?

Man: I had no experience of publishing or journalism at all. I was actually an accountant, working for a large holiday company. One day, I was reading a magazine about modern life and stress and I just said to my friends, hey, I could do better than this!

Woman: So what did you do then?

Man: Well, I spent eight months knocking on the doors of just about every big London-based publishing company hoping to find one who would discuss the project. Finally, a friend, the managing director of a big insurance company, suggested I see Tom Smith, who's the editor of the magazine *Nights Out*. He liked my ideas for the new magazine, said they were exciting, and we started to meet regularly to develop and plan its publication.

Woman: He wasn't worried about the competition?

Man: Oh no. My magazine has a completely different subject from his – we do both have the same sort of career-minded readers, but they buy our magazines for completely different reasons:

mine gives readers advice and help on how to look after themselves, how to keep fit. Of course, this sometimes includes ideas about what to do at the weekend, but his magazine is bought specifically by readers who want to know where to go and what to do in their free time – dates, places, costs, recommendations.

Woman: Mm. And who do you have working for you? Do you ask your friends to write for the magazine?

Man: Actually, I love my family and friends but the people I need, and any business needs – to be successful, are those who really know what they're doing, with the qualifications, training, experience, the lot – not necessarily well-known people, just the ones who are good at the job.

Woman: Indeed. Does the magazine now make enough money from advertising to keep going without too much outside investment?

Man: Of course not, though our advertising income is excellent. Our first copy alone brought in over twenty thousand pounds, but we're still considered a risk by the banks so we're very lucky that we have several people willing to invest in us on a personal basis. Shall I tell you how many copies of the magazine we sold last month?

Woman: Forty, fifty thousand?

Man: About seventy-five thousand. I'm really pleased sales have increased so rapidly. Apart from one month when they dropped slightly, sales have grown until they reached the seventy-five thousand mark three months ago, where they've stayed.

Woman: And how do you see the magazine developing, James, say over the next year?

Man: I'm keen to see it read by more people, of course, but that doesn't mean I want to make any great changes. It looks good now, it feels right. I'm getting all the publicity I need. All I've got to work on is getting it out to more places so that it is more widely available. At the moment, it's basically only available in London. I want to make sure everyone can buy it.

Woman: Well, good luck with that, James.

Man: Thank you.

[pause]

Now listen to the recording again.

[pause]

That is the end of Part Four. You now have ten minutes to transfer your answers to your Answer Sheet.

Note: Teacher, stop the recording here and time ten minutes. Remind students when there is **one** minute remaining.

[pause]

That is the end of the test.

Test 4 Reading

Part 1

1 B　　2 C　　3 A　　4 B　　5 A

Part 2

6 H　　7 D　　8 B　　9 E　　10 C

Part 3

11 B　　12 E　　13 G　　14 F　　15 A

Part 4

16 A　　17 C　　18 B　　19 B　　20 A
21 A　　22 C

Part 5

23 C　　24 A　　25 B　　26 B　　27 B
28 A

Part 6

29 C　　30 B　　31 C　　32 B　　33 B
34 C　　35 B　　36 A　　37 C　　38 A
39 C　　40 A

Part 7

41 SIMON HASTINGS　　42 GERMAN
43 BUSINESS (GERMAN) (FOCUS)
44 INTERMEDIATE　　45 (IN) HOTEL

Test 4   Writing

Part 1

Sample A

> Good morning,
>
> you know the project which we should ended next month. We won't be able to complete.
>
> I am so sorry but two staff members have been ill for 4 weeks now.
>
> With help for an other department we could complete it in 4 weeks.
>
> Thanks

Band 4

This response contains one or two errors; however the main problem is that the request for help (content point 3) is not sufficiently explicit – hence a Band 4.

Sample B

> My work team is scheduled to complete a project next month. I am apologising for the delay.
>
> Concerning the reason, for the delay – The project was not complete. I would need more enquiring with regards to the personnal.
> Best Regards

Band 2

Only the first content point (apology for the delay) is achieved in this script, limiting this response to a Band 2.

Part 2

Sample C

> Dear Karen Petersen
>
> I have just seen your advertisement on the newspaper. I am writing to tell you that I have a suitable building for rent.
>
> The building has an office, a big room and a bathroom. In addition, it has a telephone line and internal access which is good for you to open a internet café. It is located in the city centre and it will be available from 20th June. If you have further question, please telephone me or send an E-mail to me.
>
> I look forward to hearing from you soon.
>
> Yours sincerely

Band 5

This script achieves all the content points and uses a good range of language. The letter is well organised and generally has a positive effect on the reader.

Sample D

> Dear Miss Karen Petersen,
>
> I'm writing to informing of my own building. I saw your advertisment in the ABC business centre. I think my building might suitable for your business.
>
> My own building in 10 Oxford Street. There is a good position in London. There is 700ft on second floor. From underground station to there just 10 min on foot and there is near bus station as well.
>
> There were phone-line, light, kitchen and toilet already. There is new printing as well.
>
> My building is available now. If you need more information or you would like to visit my building, please call 020 1234 1234.
>
> Yours sincerely,

Band 3

All the content points have been achieved but there are a number of errors and little attention has been paid to text cohesion; consequently, the effect on the reader is only satisfactory.

Test 4   Listening

Part 1

1 A	2 C	3 B	4 A	5 C
6 C	7 B	8 B		

Part 2

9 XB28336
10 JOHNSTON (LIMITED/LTD)
11 60 (ROLLS)
12 CASCADE
13 21 (DAYS)
14 17 (%/PER CENT)
15 5714 (POUNDS)

Part 3

16 COMPUTING
17 RESEARCH
18 MARCH
19 OPEN NETWORK

20 (A) FLAG
21 BOSTON
22 PRODUCT (TRAINING)

Part 4

23 C	24 C	25 B	26 A	27 A
28 C	29 A	30 B		

Tapescript

Listening Test 4

This is the Business English Certificate Preliminary 2, Listening Test 4.

[pause]

Part One. Questions 1 to 8.

For questions 1–8, you will hear eight short recordings. For each question, mark one letter (A, B or C) for the correct answer.

Here is an example: Who is Emily going to write to?

[pause]

Man: Emily, that supplier we use has become very unreliable, and we've decided to look for another one.
Woman: Seems a good idea.
Man: We don't need to inform our clients, but could you send a note round to all our departments when we've decided who to replace the supplier with?
Woman: Yes, of course.

[pause]

The answer is A.

Now we are ready to start.

After you have listened once, replay each recording.

[pause]

One: Which chart shows last week's production figures?

[pause]

Man: I understand there were some problems with the production figures?
Woman: Well, there was quite a dramatic drop on Wednesday . . . because several machines broke down, and then another fall on Thursday, but after repairs, production recovered quickly and it got back to Monday's level by the end of the week.

[pause]

Two: Which floor is the Committee Room on?

[pause]

Man: Come in!
Woman: Oh . . . I think I must have the wrong room.
Man: Which room do you want?
Woman: The Committee Room. I thought it was here on the second floor.
Man: It's on the third floor and, anyway, you are lost, this is the first floor.
Woman: Oh dear, I'm sorry . . .

[pause]

Three: How many Execujet flights are there to Ireland each day?

[pause]

Woman: Execujet, the favourite airline for the business traveller, now flies to seven destinations in Ireland. With twenty-five daily departures, you have more choice, wherever you want to do business. We now fly to more than forty European destinations every day.

[pause]

Four: Which radio report is on first?

[pause]

Woman: . . . and welcome to *Business Morning*. At nine o'clock, we'll have the first of our new reports on investments, called *Money Savers*. But before that, we have *The Big Interview* with the Executive Director of INK, Martin Galway, followed by *Business News* . . .

[pause]

Five: Which is the new packaging?

[pause]

Man: I hear we've had some new packaging designed for next year's chocolate range. What's it like, d'you know?
Woman: Well, the shape of the box has changed – it's not round any more. And it's completely plain now – no pattern at all.
Man: Oh – spots are out of fashion then?
Woman: (laughs)

[pause]

Six: Which benefit will the client receive?

[pause]

Man: Well done, Karen, for winning us that contract!

Woman: Thanks. The client wanted to negotiate on everything – prices, delivery times, credit terms, and so on.

Man: And did you reduce the prices for them?

Woman: We can't affect our profit margins, so I offered them better credit terms. There's nothing more we can do to speed up delivery – it's already very fast!

[pause]

Seven: Which chart shows Freebird's market share for last year?

[pause]

Man: So how did everyone at Freebird feel about last year's market share?

Woman: Well, it's not very good news. Sales fell considerably, causing us to lose twelve and a half per cent of our market share. If we look at this chart of the four biggest producers, we can see we've lost our place as market leaders, and are now in joint second position. It's rather worrying . . .

[pause]

Eight: When will Mr Richards receive the new photocopier?

[pause]

Woman: Mr Richards, this is Maynards Office Supplies speaking. The photocopier you wanted has arrived today. We're still waiting for the other goods you ordered. They'll be here next week, but we'll deliver what we've got tomorrow. Please get back to me on . . .

[pause]

That is the end of Part One.

[pause]

Part Two. Questions 9 to 15.

Look at the quotation below.

Some information is missing.

You will hear a sales manager giving a secretary information to include in the quotation.

For each question 9–15, fill in the missing

information in the numbered space using a word, numbers or letters.

After you have listened once, replay the recording.

You have ten seconds to read through the quotation.

[pause]

Now listen, and fill in the missing information.

Woman: Hello. Jill speaking.

Man: Jill, it's Robert. I've just visited a company and I need a quotation to go in the post to them tonight. Can you do one?

Woman: Sure. If you give the details . . .

Man: OK, I'll give you a reference first. X-B-2-8-double-3-6.

Woman: Right. And who's the quotation for?

Man: Johnston Ltd. They're a new customer at Campfield Retail Park.

Woman: Is that J-O-H-N-S-T-O-N-E?

Man: No E at the end.

Woman: Right. And what is the quote for?

Man: The white patterned cotton.

Woman: We sell that in rolls of fifty metres.

Man: Well, they want three thousand metres altogether.

Woman: So I'll put down sixty then.

Man: Fine. And you'll need the product name. It's Cascade, C-A-S-C-A-D-E.

Woman: Oh yes, I know. Should I put the normal thirty days payment terms?

Man: Well, they actually wanted sixty days credit, but as they're new customers, I've insisted on twenty-one. We can review it later.

Woman: OK, fine. And, er, no discount to begin with?

Man: They originally wanted thirty per cent but we compromised on seventeen even though it's more than the fifteen we usually offer – I think they could be a good account to win.

Woman: Yes.

Man: So it should be five thousand, seven hundred and fourteen pounds altogether to pay.

Woman: Right, I've got all that. I'll make sure . . .

[pause]

Now listen to the recording again.

[pause]

That is the end of Part Two. You now have ten seconds to check your answers.

[pause]

Part Three. Questions 16 to 22.

Look at the notes about changes in a company.

Some information is missing.

You will hear part of a talk by a manager to members of staff.

For each question 16–22, fill in the missing information in the numbered space using one or two words.

After you have listened once, replay the recording.

You have ten seconds to look at the notes.

[pause]

Now listen, and write the missing words in the spaces.

Woman: Right – thanks for coming at short notice. There'll be an announcement in the media tomorrow about our planned merger, and I wanted to inform you about it first.

Now, as you all know, we've been in merger talks with two American software manufacturers, Computing International and M2C International. We nearly reached an agreement with M2C, but it was decided to go with Computing in the end.

If you're worried about job losses, I can guarantee that won't happen here at the company administration offices. The Americans want to keep our Head Office, and the production site too. The only change is to sell our research site and relocate those staff.

In fact, there are plans for all of us here at Head Office to move to a new development near the harbour, which will be ready in March next year. The actual merger takes place in May.

The major change to the new-look company is that we'll be called Open Network – er, I don't think it'll be too difficult to go from Alpha Networking to the new name.

There'll also be a new logo, and company colours will change. There was a lot of discussion about whether to keep the key as the logo, but it was decided that something different was needed, so instead it'll be a flag. Now, what about advantages for the staff? After the merger there'll still be opportunities to travel – conferences in Europe, exhibitions in Tokyo, Frankfurt, and so on, but there'll also be a staff exchange programme with the Boston office.

Another thing, of course, is that we'll have to get used to our new identity. To help us do this, starting next June, there'll be training courses. We'll be offered product training first, then the following month there'll be corporate training, and after that seminars on work skills. I'm sure these will all be very useful.

Now, before I go on, does anyone have any questions . . .

[pause]

Now listen to the recording again.

[pause]

That is the end of Part Three. You now have 20 seconds to check your answers.

[pause]

Part Four. Questions 23 to 30.

You will hear a discussion between James Pierce and Susanna White, talking about their company's current advertising campaign for a new range of convenience foods.

For each question 23–30, mark one letter (A, B or C) for the correct answer.

After you have listened once, replay the recording.

You have 45 seconds to read through the questions.

[pause]

Now listen, and mark A, B or C.

Woman: I've had some very positive feedback on the ad campaign, James.

Man: Great!

Woman: I thought you'd be interested to hear the results of a telephone survey the advertising agency carried out.

Man: Yes, very much so.

Woman: Firstly, it seems we were right to take the advice of the advertising agency and not to employ actors, as we normally do in our ads. It seems people have really responded to well-known personalities dressed as factory workers on our production line.

Man: So, did the people in the telephone survey say they felt persuaded to buy the products?

Woman: Nobody actually said that, but they definitely thought it was something different from the style of ads that's in fashion at the moment. The response that came back again and again was they hadn't seen anything like it before – they thought the ads were great.

Man: Hmm, that should really give the MD something to smile about! But what about the real question? How are sales performing?

Woman: Well, I was a little worried, because we'd set such very high targets. And sales of new products don't always perform well straight away. Also, it's such a competitive market. In fact, though, we've met all our targets so far.

Man: And maybe when more people see the ads, sales will be above target. It's only three weeks since the campaign started.

Woman: Mm, now, another interesting point is the type of consumers buying these products.

Man: We're aiming at men and women in the twenty to thirty age group, rather than teenagers.

Woman: Well, the survey showed that actually it's thirteen to nineteen year olds who buy the products more than women, and men are in third place.

Man: I wonder if that's because of the style of our ads.

Woman: Possibly. We should see whether this pattern changes as the campaign goes on.

Man: Has there been any feedback on which magazines most consumers see these ads in?

Woman: Well, *Healthy Eating* magazine has the largest number of readers, but that's not the same thing, of course. According to the survey results, *Food Ideas* was the magazine mentioned more often than any other. *Easy Meals* has been fairly successful, too, which is surprising, though that was the one the agency recommended us to advertise in.

Man: Yes, that's right. I think the agency has given us some really good advice. I'm impressed. I know it might seem that we're paying them a lot of money, but if you think of the sales we're achieving . . . after this experience, I would always use the agency – even if it costs us more.

Woman: Well, as you say, things are going very well so far.

Man: And has the agency said how long the campaign should continue for?

Woman: Yes. We've already had just about two months and the agency thinks it should go on for another month. They say we should run some new ads again later in the year, for the same length of time.

Man: OK. And are they advising us to advertise in the same publications?

Woman: The same magazines, yes. They also said we should advertise in cinema guides.

Man: Perhaps we could consider some of the popular sports magazines – convenience foods certainly suit people with busy life-styles. Anyway, advertising in some of the cinema guides is just as expensive as the national newspapers.

Woman: Well, I can go back to the agency to discuss that if you like.

Man: OK, I think that's something . . .

[pause]

Now listen to the recording again.

[pause]

That is the end of Part Four. You now have ten minutes to transfer your answers to your Answer Sheet.

Note: Teacher, stop the recording here and time ten minutes. Remind students when there is **one** minute remaining.

[pause]

That is the end of the test.

INTERLOCUTOR FRAMES

To facilitate practice for the Speaking test, the scripts that the interlocutor follows for Parts 2 and 3 appear below. They should be used in conjunction with Tests 1–4 Speaking tasks.

Interlocutor frames are not included for Part 1, in which the interlocutor asks the candidates questions directly rather than asking them to perform tasks.

Part 2: Mini presentations for two candidates (about five minutes)

Interlocutor:
- Thank you. That's the end of the first part of the test. In the next part you are each going to talk on your own.
- Now, I'm going to give each of you a card with two topics. I'd like you to choose one topic and talk about it for about one minute. You have one minute to prepare for this. You are allowed to make notes.
- All right? Here are your topics.

[Each candidate is handed a different topic card, and some paper and a pencil for notes.]

Interlocutor:
- Choose one of the topics and prepare to talk about it. Remember, you can make notes if you wish. Please don't write anything on your topic card.

[One minute's preparation time. Both candidates prepare their talks at the same time, separately.]

Interlocutor:
- All right. Now, *B, which topic have you chosen, A, or B? So would you like to show *A your topic card and talk about what you think is important when (xxx).

[B talks.]

Interlocutor:
- Thank you. Now, *A, which do you think is most important (xxx), (yyy), or (zzz)?

[A replies.]

- Thank you. All right. Now, *A, which topic have you chosen, A, or B? So would you like to show *B your topic card and talk about what you think is important when (xxx).

[A talks.]

- Thank you. Now, *B, which do you think is most important (xxx), (yyy), or (zzz)?

[B replies.]

- Thank you.

[Materials are collected.]

*USE CANDIDATES' NAMES THROUGHOUT THE TEST.

Part 3: Collaborative task and discussion (about five minutes)

Interlocutor:
- Now, in this part of the test you are going to talk about something together.
- I'm going to describe a situation.

Example: Your company is holding its annual seminar for all the sales representatives, and you are in charge of preparing the meeting room. Talk together for about two minutes about things you should provide, and decide which three things are the most important.

- Here are some ideas to help you.

[Task sheet is placed in front of the candidates so that they can both see it.]

- I'll describe the situation again.

Example: Your company is holding its annual seminar for all the sales representatives, and you are in charge of preparing the meeting room. Talk together for about two minutes about things you should provide, and decide which three things are the most important.

Now talk together. Please speak so that we can hear you.

[Candidates have about two minutes to complete the task.]

[Materials are collected.]

[Interlocutor selects one or more of the following questions as appropriate.]

Example:
- Do you think annual meetings for staff are useful? (Why/Why not?)

- What makes a meeting successful? (Why?)
- What should the person who chairs a meeting do if some participants arrive late? (Why?)
- Do you say a lot at meetings? (Why/Why not?)

- Apart from meetings, in what other ways can companies communicate with their staff? (Why?)

- Thank you. That is the end of the Speaking test.

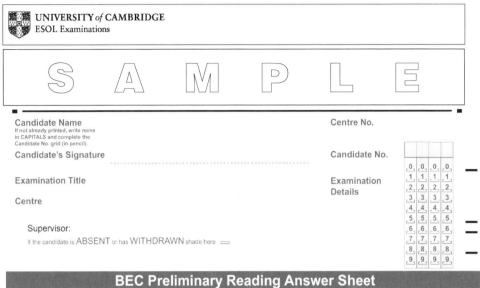

UNIVERSITY *of* **CAMBRIDGE**
ESOL Examinations

S A M P L E

Candidate Name
If not already printed, write name
in CAPITALS and complete the
Candidate No. grid (in pencil).

Candidate's Signature

Examination Title

Centre

Supervisor:
If the candidate is ABSENT or has WITHDRAWN shade here

Centre No.

Candidate No.

Examination
Details

BEC Preliminary Reading Answer Sheet

Instructions
Use a PENCIL (B or HB).
Rub out any answer you wish to change with an eraser.

For **Parts 1 to 6**:
Mark one box for each answer.

For example:
If you think C is the right answer to the question, mark your Answer Sheet like this:

0 | A B C

For **Part 7**:
Write your answer clearly in CAPITAL LETTERS.
Write one letter or number in each box.
If the answer has more than one word, leave one box empty between words.

For example:

0 Q U E S T I O N 4

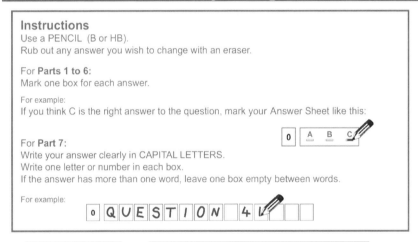

Part 1			
1	A	B	C
2	A	B	C
3	A	B	C
4	A	B	C
5	A	B	C

Part 2								
6	A	B	C	D	E	F	G	H
7	A	B	C	D	E	F	G	H
8	A	B	C	D	E	F	G	H
9	A	B	C	D	E	F	G	H
10	A	B	C	D	E	F	G	H

Turn over for Parts 3–7 ▶

Part 3

11	A	B	C	D	E	F	G	H
12	A	B	C	D	E	F	G	H
13	A	B	C	D	E	F	G	H
14	A	B	C	D	E	F	G	H
15	A	B	C	D	E	F	G	H

Part 4

16	A	B	C
17	A	B	C
18	A	B	C
19	A	B	C
20	A	B	C
21	A	B	C
22	A	B	C

Part 5

23	A	B	C
24	A	B	C
25	A	B	C
26	A	B	C
27	A	B	C
28	A	B	C

Part 6

29	A	B	C
30	A	B	C
31	A	B	C
32	A	B	C

33	A	B	C
34	A	B	C
35	A	B	C
36	A	B	C

37	A	B	C
38	A	B	C
39	A	B	C
40	A	B	C

Part 7

41

1 41 0

42

1 42 0

43

1 43 0

44

1 44 0

45

1 45 0

UNIVERSITY *of* **CAMBRIDGE**
ESOL Examinations

S A M P L E

Candidate Name
If not already printed, write name
in CAPITALS and complete the
Candidate No. grid (in pencil).

Candidate's Signature

Examination Title

Centre

Supervisor:

If the candidate is ABSENT or has WITHDRAWN shade here

Centre No.

Candidate No.

Examination
Details

0	0	0	0
1	1	1	1
2	2	2	2
3	3	3	3
4	4	4	4
5	5	5	5
6	6	6	6
7	7	7	7
8	8	8	8
9	9	9	9

BEC Preliminary Writing Answer Sheet

Part 1: Write your answer in the box below.

Write your answer to Part 2 on the other side of this sheet ▶

This section for use by Examiner only						
Part 1	0	1	2	3	4	5

Part 2: Write your answer in the box below.

This section for use by Examiner only

Part 2	0	1.1	1.2	2.1	2.2	3.1	3.2	4.1	4.2	5.1	5.2

Examiner Number

| ₀ ₁ ₂ ₃ ₄ ₅ ₆ ₇ ₈ ₉ |
| ₀ ₁ ₂ ₃ ₄ ₅ ₆ ₇ ₈ ₉ |
| ₀ ₁ ₂ ₃ ₄ ₅ ₆ ₇ ₈ ₉ |
| ₀ ₁ ₂ ₃ ₄ ₅ ₆ ₇ ₈ ₉ |

Examiner's Signature

....

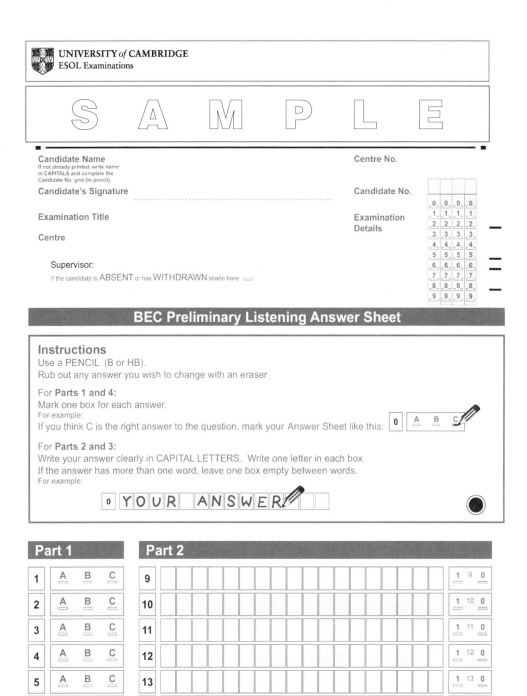

Part 3

16 1 16 0

17 1 17 0

18 1 18 0

19 1 19 0

20 1 20 0

21 1 21 0

22 1 22 0

Part 4

	A	B	C
23	A	B	C
24	A	B	C
25	A	B	C
26	A	B	C
27	A	B	C
28	A	B	C
29	A	B	C
30	A	B	C

© UCLES/K&J Photocopiable